ENDORSEMENTS

Mariel Villarreal is a true gift to the body of Christ. In *Prophetic Promises*, she welcomes us on a biblical, prophetic, personal, and profound journey into experiencing the fullness of all that God has made available to every believer.

Yes, we will face challenges, obstacles, and opposition. And we will sometimes wander in dry deserts and barren wilderness seasons. But we don't have to miss out on crossing over into our 'promised land' of fruitfulness, favor, flourishing, and fulfillment.

Mariel encourages us to co-operate with God's processes, trust His timing, and wait well on the journey. Above all, she equips us to hear the voice of God and shows how we can receive real-time revelation that will help us navigate through uncharted territory. Her personal testimonies are an inspiration and an invitation to a life of adventure.

Your God is not just a promise giver. He is a promise keeper. You don't have to live with 'hope deferred;' you can live with 'promise fulfilled.' In *Prophetic Promises*, Mariel will show you how.

- **Craig Cooney**

Lead Pastor: HOPE Church, Northern Ireland

Author of *The Tension of Transition*, *I HEAR YAHWEH*, *The Blueprint*, and *The Threshold*

Prophetic Encouragement: @daily.prophetic

The promises of God are yes and amen over our lives. God is a good Father and the divine Architect of beautiful plans for us. This book that my friend Mariel has written is a culmination of entering into God's promises and being able to hear the Father's voice for ourselves. It's the essence of staying on course and running our race that the Lord has set for us. Mariel is a skilled author and teacher of the Holy Spirit and how to follow His leading. She is a much-needed and trusted prophetic voice for the times we live in, and her heart is fully devoted to the Lord. I know and pray that this book will lead you into a deeper encounter with the Lord Jesus.

- Alwyn Uys
Author of *Unbroken*
Founder of Alwyn Uys Ministries

It's such a great honor to endorse the book, Prophetic Promises. I've known Mariel for over a decade and have seen her grow in her prophetic gifting while remaining humble and reliant on the Lord. The wisdom found in this book has been cultivated through her own faith journey with God and through the tests she has faced personally. I encourage you to not only read this book but continually ask the Lord how He is calling you to respond to the various chapters and sections. I believe that if you invite God to speak to you through this book and have the courage to apply what He says, your life will never be the same.

- Andrew Chalmers
Author of *Discovering the Joy*
Founder of Harvest Movement

One of the most disorienting realities in the life of faith is living in two places at once—rooted in the promises of God while standing waist-deep in the wilderness. But God invites us into a beautiful story of intimacy, invitation, and wonder as we learn to hold both simultaneously, and ultimately choose to let one win out. That's the triumph that Mariel reveals to us in *Prophetic Promises*, as she invites us to follow her journey and the journey of God's people throughout time to inherit what is rightfully theirs through Christ.

I've known Mariel for close to ten years and have the joy of walking with her as her pastor. The most beautiful part of this book is that it showcases the kind of life I've watched Mariel live. There's no fluff here; it's genuine and sincere and true to her process with Jesus. Her journey with the Lord has been a gift to me and to our church family, and she is a gift to the Body as a prophetic voice and friend.

I pray as you read this book, you too will discover the treasure chest of tools and prophetic wisdom she shares and how to contend for every promise God gives. "For no matter how many promises God has made, they are "Yes" in Christ." 2 Corinthians 1:20

- Grant Collins
Lead Pastor, Fountain City Church

In a world filled with uncertainty, *Prophetic Promises* stands as a beacon of hope, guiding readers on a profound journey of seeking God's promises. Through its pages, Mariel Villarreal masterfully weaves together biblical truths, personal anecdotes, and practical wisdom to empower readers to uncover the fulfillment of God's promises in their lives.

This book is not merely a collection of theories but a roadmap for those hungering for the manifestation of God's prophetic words. With depth and clarity, Mariel navigates the intricacies of seeking God's face, cultivating intimacy with Jesus, and partnering with Him to see His promises come to pass.

Whether you're grappling with doubt, facing delays, or simply longing for a deeper connection with God, *Prophetic Promises* offers invaluable insights and strategies to propel you forward. Through heartfelt encouragement and practical teachings, you will be equipped to overcome obstacles, embrace patience, and stand in faith as you await God's promises. Let this book be your guide as you journey toward a deeper understanding of God's faithfulness and a greater experience of His prophetic fulfillment in your life.

- Dr. Diane Swanson
Christian Leadership Coach
Author of *The Leadership Mantle*
National Women's Program Director, Hoving Home

PROPHETIC PROMISES

PROPHETIC PROMISES

**Navigating Your Adventure
To God's Promises**

MARIEL VILLARREAL

© 2024 by Mariel Villarreal

www.marielvillarreal.com

All rights reserved. No part of this publication may be reproduced, distributed, or transmitted in any form or by any means, including photocopying, recording, or other electronic or mechanical methods, without the prior written permission of the publisher, except in the case of brief quotations embodied in critical reviews and certain other noncommercial uses permitted by copyright law.

Unless otherwise indicated, Scripture quotations are from the Holy Bible, New International Version®, NIV®. Copyright © 1973, 1978, 1984, 2011 by Biblica, Inc.™ Used by permission of Zondervan. All rights reserved worldwide. Scripture quotations marked (NLT) are taken from the Holy Bible, New Living Translation, copyright © 1996, 2004, 2015 by Tyndale House Foundation. Used by permission of Tyndale House Publishers, Inc., Carol Stream, Illinois 60188. All rights reserved. Scripture quotations marked (ESV) are taken from The Holy Bible, English Standard Version® (ESV®), copyright © 2001 by Crossway, a publishing ministry of Good News Publishers. Used by permission. All rights reserved. Scripture quotations marked (NKJV) are taken from the New King James Version®. Copyright © 1982 by Thomas Nelson. Used by permission. All rights reserved. Scripture quotations marked (BSB) are taken from the Berean Study Bible. © 2016, 2018 by Bible Hub. Used by permission. All rights reserved worldwide. Scripture quotations marked (TPT) are from The Passion Translation®. Copyright © 2017, 2018 by Passion & Fire Ministries, Inc. Used by permission. All rights reserved. ThePassionTranslation.com. Scripture quotations marked (MSG) are taken from THE MESSAGE, copyright © 1993, 1994, 1995, 1996, 2000, 2001, 2002 by Eugene H. Peterson. Used by permission of NavPress. All rights reserved. Represented by Tyndale House Publishers, Inc. Scripture quotations marked (GW) are taken from the Holy Bible, GOD'S WORD®, © 1995 God's Word to the Nations. Used by permission of God's Word Mission Society. All rights reserved.

ISBN 978-1-964471-03-7 (Paperback)

ISBN 978-1-964471-00-6 (HC)

ISBN 978-1-964471-01-3 (E-Book)

Cover design by Studio Grason

Some names and details included in this book have been changed to protect the identity of individuals mentioned.

To my father,
Francisco Javier Villarreal,

You wrote in my baby book
Before you left this world
That I would
"Change the world"

I hope you can see from the
balcony of Heaven,
This is your legacy.

To my heavenly Father,

When you're not dancing with me,
You are cheering me on from the wings.
Thank you for this divine dance with You.

CONTENTS

INTRODUCTION: POMEGRANATES OF PROMISE — 15

PART 1: THE POWER OF A PROPHETIC PROMISE — 21
Made to Hear His Voice..23
The Voice of the Good Shepherd...................................32
Your Prophetic Promises...39

PART 2: OUR PROMISE MAKER — 47
Our Promise Maker..49
Pregnant with Promise..54
To the Promise Carrier..59
Prophetic Promise Carriers...61
Protect Your Promise...65
Expect the Unexpected..69
Make Room for the Promise...73
In the Middle..77
Your Due Time is Coming...81

PART 3: WILDERNESS WONDERS — 85
A Vision of a Promised Land..87
Cloud by Day, Fire by Night...93
Miracle Manna...98
Our Bread of Life...103
Sign Language..107
The Sign of the Praying Mantis....................................110
The Sign of the Cardinal...116
My Hidden Manna...122
Wonder Upon Wonder..126

PART 4: JUST IN TIME   129
God's Perfect Timing..131
The Issachar Anointing... 135
The Waiting Room...140
Midnight Hour Miracles... 144
Midnight Oil...149
Darkest Before the Dawn..154
3 Kinds of Spiritual Delays....................................... 158
Divine Interruptions... 169
For Such a Time as This... 174
Trust His Timing..178

PART 5: PROPHESY THE PROMISE   181
Did God Really Say?...183
Prophesy the Promise...187
A Great Test...193
Wait for the True Promise..197
Don't Tease Me..202
Forget-Me-Not...205
Where You Go, I Will Go..210
Bittersweet: Naomi's Story....................................... 214
God Will Bless the Broken Road..............................218

PART 6: GOLD REFINED BY FIRE   223
Refiner's Image...225
From the Pit to the Palace..228
The Lord Will Provide...232
A Heavy Carriage Load..236

Wrestling vs. Resting for the Promise..241
Discerning God's Voice...245
God, Is This From You?..253
Warfare at the Door of Destiny...257
2222: Doors of Destiny..262
Become a Living Sacrifice..268
Fourth Man in the Fire 272

PART 7: ENTER THE PROMISED LAND 275

Pomegranates of Promise...277
God's Good Report..286
Rumors of Giants...290
Emboldened...296
The Miracle is in Your Movement..301
Pioneers, Cross over!...303
Crossing My Jordan...305
Keep the Testimony Alive..309
Take the City..313
Every Promise Fulfilled..317
Fruit Bearers...324
Our True Treasure...329

AFTERWARD: THE FINAL SIGN OF THE CARDINAL 333
A PRAYER OF SURRENDER 337
ACKNOWLEDGEMENTS 339
NOTES 341

INTRODUCTION
POMEGRANATES OF PROMISE

> *For the Lord your God is bringing you into a good land—a land with brooks, streams, and deep springs gushing out into the valleys and hills; a land with wheat and barley, vines and fig trees, pomegranates, olive oil and honey ...*
> **Deuteronomy 8:7-9**

One night in August of 2020, I had a dream from God I will never forget.

At midnight, a friend picked me up from my house in her Jeep. Windows down, I rode in the passenger seat as she drove us to some unknown destination. I remember feeling a cool breeze as we moved through the night, so tangible it felt like it wasn't a dream. I felt carefree and content—the opposite of how I felt in my waking life.

In reality, I felt deeply hopeless. After years of praying for my promises from God to come to pass, I saw no signs of a breakthrough. Yet, God kept leading me to believe he wasn't finished with my story. He kept confirming his word to me through consistent signs and wonders. After years of my journey, I was tired of contending in faith and staying on his narrow path. I felt like giving up for the thousandth time.

Then, I had this dream ...

Suddenly, I realized my friend had driven us to a graveyard with just enough dim moonlight to see around us. She parked the Jeep on top of a tombstone. Something caught my eye in front of the grave. This was the reason she brought me here.

Peering through the twilight, I saw a bush full of fruit growing from the grave, gently rustling in the breeze.

I drew in for a closer look. The fruit was unlike anything I had ever seen—it was shaped like a simple crown as if a child had designed it. It glowed in the dark.

"This is exactly what I wanted!" I said as tears welled up in my eyes. I felt a deep sense of wonder and gratitude in my heart. However, in my natural mind, I didn't understand why the fruit was so meaningful to me. *Why was I moved to tears?*

Then, the scene switched, and I saw the fruit served on a table for Thanksgiving.

I woke up from the dream, amazed. Not every dream is from God, but as you walk with the Holy Spirit, you can grow in the gifts of discernment and interpretation to understand the messages he gives in the night seasons. This was no ordinary dream. I knew God had just spoken to me.

If God was speaking, what was he saying?

I Spy

Later that day, as I stepped out the door to take my dog, Sebastian, on a walk, something caught my eye in the distant field across the street.

Are those bushes full of … fruit?

My heart began to pound with excitement as I went to explore. I was visiting my mother that week; she had lived across from this field for over a decade. It belonged to a church, and I had gone on many prayer walks talking to Jesus there over the years.

The bushes had never borne fruit to my knowledge … until now.

As I drew nearer, I saw more clearly.

Pomegranates. The two bushes were full of pomegranates. At least *twenty* of them! I picked one and saw a crown shape adorning it—exactly like the crown from my dream. Waves of wonder and awe surged through me. Jesus was showing me a sign to confirm the dream he had given me.

From that day on, God began to reveal a special prophetic message through my dream. I want to give you a sneak peek of the meaning of the pomegranate, which I will unpack even more later on this journey with you.

Sneak Peek of the Promises of God

> *When they reached the Valley of Eshkol, they cut off a branch bearing a single cluster of grapes. Two of them carried it on a pole between them, along with some pomegranates and figs.* **Numbers 13:23**

When Joshua and Caleb returned from spying on the promised land, they gave the children of Israel a preview of the blessings in store: grapes, figs, and pomegranates.

Through my dream and the pomegranates in the field, God was giving me a special prophetic message. I was spying on the fruit of the promised land, not just for me but for his people. God's promises are up ahead—nearer now than ever before.

Many have spent years wandering wildernesses and pruning seasons, waiting for God's word to come to pass in their lives. We can feel like we are in an endless waiting room for a promise far past its due date, having taken every step of obedience and faith we know to take, only to be left wondering, *Where is the fulfillment? Will I ever reach my promised land?*

But God does not make a promise without bringing it to pass. The promises that seem barren and dead in the grave will experience the resurrection power of Christ—even at the final midnight hour.

God is a miracle worker, after all.

As sure as the pomegranates bloomed and glowed in the dark in my dream, God's promises are alive and active today. Although a deep darkness covers the earth in this time, his glory will shine through our lives as he bears the beautiful fruit of promise in our lives.

I spied the pomegranate of promise. It was not just a sign for me but for the body of Christ. We will see the fulfillment of new and long-awaited prophetic promises unfold with our own eyes. It's time to enter the promised land.

> *Is there yet any seed left in the barn? Until now, the vine and the fig tree, the pomegranate and the olive tree have not borne fruit.*
> *"'From this day on I will bless you.'"*
> **Haggai 2:19**

Adventure Awaits

A promise from God is an invitation to a wildly wonderful adventure. Are you ready to take the next step towards your promised land?

While the path to God's promises is a narrow way that few choose to travel on, you aren't like everyone else. You are called. You are chosen. You are set apart for such a time as this.

Deep in your heart, you know Jesus is calling you forward into every blessing he has for you.

Use this devotional book as a field guide, a treasure map, as you travel along the path God has marked for you. When you get lost and feel like your faith is faltering, open these pages again. Anchor yourself in the truth of God's word and remind yourself of the promises he has spoken to you.

Your promises from God await you.

Let's start the journey together.

PART I
THE POWER OF A PROPHETIC PROMISE

*Building a Foundation to
Receive a Promise from God*

MADE TO HEAR HIS VOICE

> *Here I am! I stand at the door and knock. If anyone hears my voice and opens the door, I will come in and eat with that person, and they with me.*
> **Revelation 3:20**

A prophetic promise is not your typical kind of promise. It's a special word given to you by God about the unique plans he has for you and your destiny.

To receive a prophetic promise, you must first understand a foundational truth: you were made to hear God's voice.

Let that sink in for a moment.

The living God of the whole universe wants to speak with you. He wants an audience with you—yes, *you*. He will clear his schedule every time you call. He will hush all of heaven when you lift your voice in prayer.

Not only can you hear *from* God, but you are invited to talk *with* him. This is a special invitation to divine friendship with the King of Kings.

To become someone's friend, we must pursue a relationship with them. Simply put, relationships require communication. This involves not just praying—talking *to* God—but listening for his response. Friendship is built on a back-and-forth dialogue, a heart-to-heart exchange.

Jesus wants to *know* you intimately. The word intimacy means *into-me-you-see*. He wants to see into every corner of your heart. I believe we move Jesus when we invite him into the most valuable and vulnerable areas of our lives—from the precious and painful to the secret and scary, the sacred and sloppy.

God cares about your every dream, desire, worry, and burden. What matters to you matters to him. He is not surprised by your messes or mistakes. There is nothing you could share with him that would shock him, overwhelm him, or make him love you any less. He created you for this hour in history, with a fingerprint unlike any other. He delights to give you the desires of your heart.

Jesus loves you more than you can imagine. Today, right now. Right here. Fully, wholly, completely. Extravagantly.

As you start this adventure to your promised land, Jesus is standing at the door, inviting you to sit and talk with him. As you open the door of your heart to him, he will open his heart to you and reveal the plans he created you for. He wants to give you hope and a future—prophetic promises for your life.

How did this beautiful invitation to friendship begin? Let's take a look at the very start of the story.

Our Story: Back to the Garden

> *Then the man and his wife heard the voice of the LORD God walking in the garden in the breeze of the day.*
> **Genesis 3:8 BSB**

It all started in a garden—the Garden of Eden.

Enter Adam and Eve—the first of humankind.

They walked in perfect union with God, talking with him in the cool of the day. They knew God as an intimate friend, and he knew them.

In their nakedness, they were fully known and loved by their Creator.

Eden was a picture of what we were made for: divine friendship with God.

However, we know how the story goes. Through Adam and Eve's free will choices, sin entered the world. One tempting bite from the tree of the knowledge of good and evil, and just like that, the perfect relationship between God and humankind was torn.

From that moment on, we see broken people trying to make their way back to a perfect God. Throughout the Old Testament, the children of Israel faced the consequences of the fall of man.

They lacked direct access to their heavenly Father.

They relied on prophets to communicate with God for them.

They needed a high priest to atone for their sins every year.

They could not keep God's commandments or the religious laws of men— they kept falling short again and again. All of their efforts were never enough. Yet, there was still hope.

God gave a great prophetic promise: a perfect Savior—a Messiah—to save people from their sins and restore them to a right relationship with him. This was a promise not just for the nation of Israel—but for the world.

Finally, the promise came when Jesus Christ, the Anointed One, arrived on the scene. John the Baptist proclaimed of him, "Behold, the Lamb of God, who takes away the sin of the world!" (John 1:29 ESV)

He was no longer a faraway-kind-of-God but an up-close-and-personal Savior. His name is Emmanuel, God with Us.

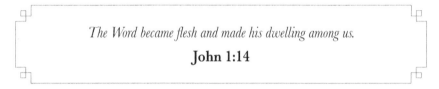

The Word became flesh and made his dwelling among us.
John 1:14

In a second garden, the garden of Gethsemane, Jesus willingly laid down his will for the will of the Father. He was on a mission to restore us back to God.

Jesus atoned for our sins once and for all with the shedding of his innocent blood. The moment he gave up his spirit on the cross, the veil of separation in the temple was torn, marking the remaking of a holy friendship between God and his people.

When Jesus rose from the grave three days later, he appeared first to Mary Magdalene in a third garden—the garden tomb.

In the original setting where our relationship with God was once broken, we were restored to God in a new garden. It was a full-circle redemption.

Afterward, Jesus ascended into heaven and sent the Holy Spirit at Pentecost. On that day, God poured out his Spirit on his people, filling them with power and boldness to be witnesses to the nations.

The Holy Spirit is now available to the people of God every single day of our lives.

We can now enter a personal relationship with Jesus Christ and boldly approach his throne of grace with confidence in our time of need (Hebrews 4:16).

We no longer need an earthly priest or prophet to act as a mediator between us and our Heavenly Father. We can enter the presence of God anytime, anywhere.

> *For there is one God and one mediator between God and mankind, the man Christ Jesus, who gave himself as a ransom for all people.*
> **1 Timothy 2:5-6**

We have made our way back to the garden. What a beautiful privilege and honor we have been given to know God intimately as a Savior, a perfect heavenly Father, a returning Bridegroom King … A friend.

God is Still Speaking

> *"'In the last days,' God says, I will pour out my Spirit on all people. Your sons and daughters will prophesy, your young men will see visions, your old men will dream dreams."*
> **Acts 2:17**

God fulfilled a powerful prophetic promise on the day of Pentecost: the Holy Spirit was poured out on all people. The sound of a great rushing wind filled the upper room. Tongues of fire fell. The disciples began to prophesy, speak in tongues, and declare the works of God, astounding those who witnessed the moment. The good news of the Gospel of Jesus Christ began to spread like wildfire to the ends of the earth.

Of all things that could mark an outpouring of the Holy Spirit, have you ever wondered why God chose to release prophecy, dreams, visions, signs, and wonders as described in Acts chapter 2? I believe the answer is simple yet profound: these are all unique ways we can hear from God. Our God's supernatural means of communication advanced his kingdom in a lost and broken world, so that everyone who calls on his name may be saved.

Not only is God still pouring out his Spirit, but he is still speaking today. We need to hear him for our lives and the world around us for such a time as this.

We are living in an Isaiah 60-like era, where light clashes with darkness. Although deep darkness covers the earth, it is a sign God's glory is going to radiate through his people.

"Arise, shine, for your light has come,

    and the glory of the Lord rises upon you.

See, darkness covers the earth

    and thick darkness is over the peoples,

but the Lord rises upon you

    and his glory appears over you.

Nations will come to your light,

    and kings to the brightness of your dawn."

Isaiah 60:1-3

Our generation reminds me of the times Charles Dickens described in his book *A Tale of Two Cities*: "It was the best of times, it was the worst of times, it was the age of wisdom, it was the age of foolishness, it was the epoch of belief, it was the epoch of incredulity, it was the season of light, it was the season of darkness, it was the spring of hope, it was the winter of despair."

In this hour, we have a choice to embrace hope or despair. We can fuel our hearts with belief or unbelief.

Every day, many voices bombard us, telling us what to think, how to live, and whom to believe—from our families and communities to the news and media to the enemy of our souls, and many other sources. Whether positive or negative, for better or for worse, hopeful or harmful, these voices speak their own report about our past, present, and future.

Ultimately, it comes down to a powerful choice we have been given: who will we listen to? What report will we believe?

Above all the noise, we must discern the voice of our Heavenly Father. His heart is for us, and he longs to reveal his plans for us that he designed before we were born.

Jesus Christ is the God of all hope, and despite the intimidating reports of giants in the land, he is broadcasting his own report. No matter how deep the darkness is, he wants to release redemption in the nations. He has promises stored up to release in this generation that will reveal his glory to the nations when they are fulfilled in our lives.

The prophetic promise of the outpouring of the Holy Spirit didn't end at Pentecost. It's an open invitation for us to receive today. As God pours out his Spirit on all people in this time, one of the results will be the gift of prophecy: hearing God through dreams, visions, signs, wonders, and boldly declaring his truth. Listening to his voice and obeying him empowers us to rise above the negative news of the world and fulfill his mission on the earth.

God is still speaking today, and he longs to talk with us as a loving Father, a Wonderful Counselor, and a faithful Friend.

When we truly believe this, we begin to expect to hear from him. Our hearts get positioned in faith to receive his words. As we pursue friendship with Jesus, our Good Shepherd, his voice will lead us forward into his promises for our lives.

REFLECTION

- Do you believe God wants to speak to you today?
- What voices are loudest to you in this season? Are they speaking hope or despair over your past, present, and future?
- How can you build deeper friendship with Jesus today?

Dear Heavenly Father,

I pray for you to pour out your Spirit in my life! Open my heart and my eyes to see how you are speaking all of the time. Help me to recognize your voice above all of the noise. I want to hear the good report you are speaking over my prophetic promises, my promised land from you. Fill my heart with fresh hope and faith as I continue on this adventure with you. I want to know you even more deeply as an intimate friend. In Jesus' name, amen.

THE VOICE OF THE GOOD SHEPHERD

> *"My sheep hear my voice, and I know them, and they follow me."*
> **John 10:27 ESV**

If God is still speaking, what does his voice sound like?

Jesus described our relationship with him through a parable, portraying himself as a Good Shepherd and his followers as his flock. In John 10:14, Jesus said, "I am the good shepherd; I know my sheep and my sheep know me."

The word "know" in this passage is the Greek word *ginosko*.[1] It means "to know through personal experience (first-hand acquaintance)." We are created to know and be known by God through first-hand, personal experience.

In Jesus' time, a shepherd would spend day in and day out with his flock. Daily proximity and time with their shepherd made his sheep intimately familiar with him. His sheep knew their leader's voice so well that he could sound a unique call to his flock while they grazed with other sheepfolds, and his own would come running one by one.[2]

In the same way, Jesus calls us to stay close to him all day, every day. In this place of consistent friendship and connection, we begin to recognize the voice of our Good Shepherd above the rest.

In the parable, Jesus doesn't say, "My sheep rarely hear my voice, and I am going to make it difficult for them to understand me." He also doesn't say, "Only my super-spiritual sheep hear me—so good luck to the rest of you!"

No—hearing God is meant to be a basic part of being in his sheepfold. Relationship with Jesus is a right given to the sons and daughters in the family of God.

As our Good Shepherd, Jesus is communicating, "It's not supposed to be confusing and complicated to hear my voice. You just need to come close and spend time with me. Get to know my gentle nature and the loving way I lead and protect you. Talk with me. Abide with me."

Discerning His Voice

> *"But they will never follow a stranger; in fact, they will run away from him because they do not recognize a stranger's voice."*
> **John 10:5**

While Jesus made it clear that his followers can easily recognize his voice, he also drew attention to another voice his sheep may encounter—the voice of the thief. Jesus said, "The thief comes only to steal and kill and destroy; I have come that they may have life, and have it to the full" (John 10:10).

How do we distinguish God's voice from the deceitful whispers of the thief, the enemy of our souls? First, we can use the written Word to grow in discernment. In Matthew 7:15-20, Jesus said we can judge a tree by its fruit. The "tree" represents the source of the message, while the "fruit" symbolizes its impact on our lives. Good trees bear good fruit and bad trees bear bad fruit.

Are the voices you listen to causing you to produce the fruits of the Holy Spirit listed in Galatians: "the fruit of the Spirit is love, joy, peace, forbearance, kindness, goodness, faithfulness, gentleness and self-control" (Gal. 5:22-23)? When a voice causes you to yield one of these attributes—that's good fruit!

On the other hand, are the voices speaking into your life stealing your joy and causing you to feel hopeless, discouraged, and depressed? Unbelief, fear, and foreboding are fruits of the thief. While God may correct us if we get of course in life, he will not speak words of condemnation or shame. [3]

When you identify rotten fruit, you need to stand firm in your identity as a child of God and take spiritual authority over the lies coming to steal from you.

God's voice may sound like, "There is so much hope for your future. I have beautiful plans for you, and you will persevere through this trial. In your weakness, I am made strong." He is releasing hope, even in the darkest night. He corrects us to protect us and guide us on the right paths he has for us. His voice drips with overwhelming love for us.

On the other hand, the thief may say, "The future is bleak. Nothing will ever change. God won't come through for you. You have nothing to look forward to in life." The enemy echoes despair, fear, and hopelessness, attempting to get us to doubt God's goodness and truth.

We need to pay attention to the voices we lend our ears to and the reports we choose to believe. So often, God's voice will come in the form of a still, small whisper—as quiet as a thought.[4] In a similar way, the thief can disguise his lies as seemingly innocent thoughts. However, these subtle thoughts, positive or negative, can sow seeds that produce fruit in us over time.

Our thoughts shape our beliefs. Our beliefs dictate our decisions. Our decisions lead to actions. Our actions create the trajectory of our lives.[5] Therefore, we must "guard our heart above all else, for it determines the course of your life" (Proverbs 4:23 NLT).

This is why we need to test the fruit of the thoughts we think and the voices that speak. We must come into agreement with hope for our future—and reject any words that yield rotten fruit in our lives.

We must grow in our ability to hear God's voice—the voice of the Good Shepherd who laid down his life for us.

7 Simple Ways to Grow in Hearing God's Voice

Let's explore seven simple ways to grow in hearing God's voice. Throughout this journey, I will share more insight in several of the following areas.

1. Time

Spend time with Jesus. Cultivate a sacred, secret space to seek him regularly. Create a prayer closet or make your car an altar during your commute. Lean into his presence during the busyness of your day. Practice being still before him. Turn off screens and schedule daily appointments to build friendship with Jesus.

2. **Proximity**

   Worship and gratitude are powerful ways to enter God's presence. Discover what brings you close to him—whether it's taking a walk, playing music, painting, or another activity. Make a gratitude list of the blessings in your life. Remember, "Draw near to God, and he will draw near to you" (James 4:8 ESV).

3. **Grow in the Word**

   Invest time in reading your Bible and studying the nature of God revealed in Jesus Christ. The more you let the Holy Spirit write the written Word upon your heart, the stronger your discernment will grow to know his voice.

3. **Ask God Questions**

   Ask God questions to jumpstart a conversation and pause to listen for his response. Lay down your own agenda and open your heart to hear what is on God's mind. For example, you can ask, "Holy Spirit, what is on your heart today?" or "Father God, what are you teaching me in this season?" or "Jesus, what do you desire to do in my life this week?"

4. **Journal His Voice**

   Journaling what God says to you will sharpen your ability to hear him. Refer back to your journal entries and test them against the Bible. Over time, you can check to see if God has given you confirmation on what you recorded. Plus, journaling is a great way to keep track of answered prayers.

5. **Grow in Understanding God's Language**

   God speaks in many different ways. He uses the creative language of his written Word, signs, wonders, miracles, visions, dreams, prophetic words, his creation, and more. When God speaks through these supernatural means, he invites us to learn how to interpret his messages. Throughout this journey, I will share different examples of ways God communicates.

6. **Godly Community**

   Inviting a godly, trustworthy community into the process of discerning God's voice is a powerful key. Allowing others to evaluate what we think God is speaking fosters a safe space to grow in hearing the Lord for ourselves and one another.

7. **Develop Discernment and Test the Fruit**

   Pray for discernment as you listen for his voice. Study the Bible and the nature of Jesus and ask God to help you test the fruit of what you discern. Hold onto the good fruit and throw out the rotten fruit. Pray over what you hear from God and ask for confirmation and feedback from those you trust.

As we continue on this path to God's prophetic promises, refer to these seven simple steps to amplify your ability to hear his voice. As you cultivate your relationship with Jesus, you'll grow in greater discernment to recognize his voice above all the rest.

REFLECTION

- How can you cultivate your ability to hear God in your daily life this season?

- How can you discern God's voice from the enemy's voice?

- Do you recognize any seeds of doubt the enemy has been sowing in your life? Do you discern any words of hope God is speaking to you?

- Spend fifteen minutes with Jesus today, and ask him, "What's on your heart today?" Listen for his response and write it down.

Dear Lord Jesus,

I want to know your voice, Good Shepherd! Help me grow in discernment to recognize and follow your voice. Thank you for helping me to guard my heart and mind against the deception of the thief. As I listen to you and follow you, I pray my life will yield abundantly good fruit. Amen.

YOUR PROPHETIC PROMISES

Call to me and I will answer you, and will tell you great and hidden things that you have not known.
Jeremiah 33:3 NLT

God longs to speak to you and reveal his purposes for you. In fact, I believe he wants to speak to you even more than you want to hear a word from him. He desires to give you promises to fill you with overflowing hope for your life.

The term "prophetic promises" refers to promises given from the heart of God for the future. To understand the nature of a prophetic promise, let's look at the function of the prophetic gift.

Gift of Prophecy

In the New Testament, Paul encourages us to passionately desire prophecy, because it gives strength, encouragement, and comfort to God's people.[6] He also declares, "For you can all prophesy in turn so that everyone may be instructed and encouraged" (1 Corinth. 14:31).

The word "prophesy" comes from the Greek word *prophēteuó* (prof-ate-yoo'-o), meaning "to express God's thoughts, heart, will, and intentions." It involves predicting future events (foretelling) or asserting God's will (forthtelling).[7]

Let's simplify this: As we draw closer to Jesus, his voice becomes clearer. As we hear him, we share what the Holy Spirit reveals—either foreseeing future events or declaring God's heart.

Here are two facets[8] of a prophetic promise:

1. **Foretelling** (prediction): In Genesis 41-42, Joseph's two prophetic dreams of ruling over his family come true.

2. **Forthtelling** (asserting God's intentions): In Ezekiel 37, God instructed Ezekiel to prophesy life to dry, dead bones, transforming them into a living army.

When we receive a prophetic promise from God, he shows us what is coming *before it happens.* In John 16:13 (NLT), Jesus explained that the Holy Spirit's role in our lives includes this function: "When the Spirit of truth comes, he will guide you into all truth. He will not speak on his own but will tell you what he has heard. He will tell you about the future."

At times, God may call us to prophesy a promise—we speak life to dry bones. Like Ezekiel, we partner with the Lord to declare forth and pray for the outcome he has shown us by divine inspiration.

Embracing God's prophetic promises involves not only receiving insights for the future but also partnering with him in faith to fulfill his intended outcomes. As we deepen our relationship with Jesus and eagerly pursue spiritual gifts, especially prophecy, we position ourselves to receive his prophetic promises.

Hope for the Future

> *May the God of hope fill you with all joy and peace as you trust in him, so that you may overflow with hope by the power of the*
> **Holy Spirit. Romans 15:13**

On this journey, we must remember we serve the God of all hope, who wants to strengthen, encourage, and comfort us. His words and promises for us will align with these values. Even when we face a trial, storm, or difficulty, he has a redemptive plan to bring us through. He is a Good Shepherd, leading us on the right paths for our lives.

> *Yahweh is my best friend and my shepherd.*
> *I always have more than enough.*
> *He offers a resting place for me in his luxurious love.*
> *His tracks take me to an oasis of peace near the quiet brook of bliss.*
> *That's where he restores and revives my life.*
> *He opens before me the right path and*
> *leads me along in his footsteps of righteousness.*
> **Psalm 23:1-3 TPT**

As we spend time with God, he will show us his plans for us and those around us—our families, communities, cities, and nations. These beautiful treasures become our prophetic promises. They demonstrate the delight of a heavenly Father who loves to be involved in the intricate details of our lives.

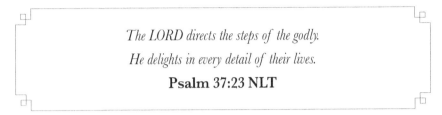

*The LORD directs the steps of the godly.
He delights in every detail of their lives.*
Psalm 37:23 NLT

These special promises are not empty words or merely wishful thinking. Prophetic promises are the very blueprints of heaven for our lives.

Prophetic Promises Blueprints

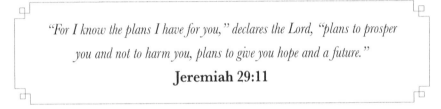

"For I know the plans I have for you," declares the Lord, "plans to prosper you and not to harm you, plans to give you hope and a future."
Jeremiah 29:11

God gave the children of Israel a wonderful prophetic promise. He spoke of a coming Promised Land, a vision of hope for their future.

In giving this promise, he showed them a heavenly blueprint: a land flowing with milk and honey, abundant with good fruit.

Just as the Israelites received a vision of their Promised Land, so too are we invited to envision the fulfillment of God's promises in our lives.

Whether you desire a promise from the Lord, or already hold one close to your heart, it's time to receive fresh hope for the future.

Let's pursue God for a blueprint for your prophetic promises.

Activation: Chart Your Prophetic Promises

Welcome to this prophetic prayer activation designed to help you connect with God's heart and receive his promises for your life. Take this opportunity to set aside dedicated time to envision and pray over your promised land. Find a secret, quiet place and prepare your heart for holy conversation with Jesus.

Begin by asking God to reveal his promises for you in specific areas. While I've listed some areas below, remain open to any areas the Holy Spirit may highlight to you during your prayer time:

- Your Relationship with Jesus
- Your Calling
- Your Relationships
- Your Family
- Your Marriage
- Your Health
- Your Spiritual Growth
- Your Ministry
- Your Finances
- Your Career
- Your Desires
- Your Gifts and Talents
- Your Community (church, workplace, school, etc.)
- Your City
- Your Nation

Prophetic Promise Conversation Prompts

Use the following questions to kickstart the conversation with Jesus. I encourage you to journal your reflections and record what God speaks to you.

- "Jesus, will you reveal the promise you have for me in this area?"
- "What hope and blessing are you speaking over this area?"
- "Will you remind me of the promises you have already spoken?"
- "What steps of action or obedience do I need to take to partner with you in faith for this promise?"
- "Lord God, would you show me an area I am experiencing the most hopelessness? What promise are you speaking over this part of my life?"

As you pray over each area, be still and listen for the voice of the Holy Spirit. You may hear his subtle whisper, see a vision, or receive a Bible verse. God may even give you a dream as you seek him. Ask him to explain more about what he shows you.

If you received specific Bible verses, prophetic words, dreams, visions, or confirmations about these promises, write them down. You may even choose to create a vision board for your promised land.

Lastly, I encourage you to ask God this important question about your promises: "Heavenly Father, will you show me how this promise will make an impact for your kingdom?"

Write down the vision and pray over it with an expectant heart.

As you spend time with Jesus, he may reveal new prophetic promises for you or stir your heart to remember words he has already spoken. I encourage you to dream big with the Lord, and set doubt on the shelf during this prayer activation. Allow your heart room to breathe in Jesus' words of abundant life.

You may catch God's fresh vision for your calling—a deep sense of purpose to make an impact for his kingdom. He may speak to you about a plan for breakthrough in your family, marriage, or relationships. You may develop a new dream to launch into your calling, ministry, business, or creative idea. He may reveal a redemptive plan for a prodigal to return home, new life after a time of loss, or restoration in health or finances. He may speak of turnarounds, solutions, new beginnings, reconciliations, or the resurrection of dreams. He may breathe life to impossible situations in need of a miracle.

On a broader scale, he may give you vision to see a powerful move of God in your city. He may show you how to partner with his plans for awakening and revival, to put an end to darkness and injustice, and for the gospel to spread to the ends of the earth—starting in your own neighborhood.

The good news is that God has a plan for every area of our lives, in every season. He is a Restorer and Redeemer. He is a Father of Heavenly lights who gives good gifts to his children. There is nothing too impossible for him. He is writing a beautiful plan for your life.

He is calling you to step into his prophetic promises—the promised land he has for your life.

On this journey we will explore the journey from a promise given to a promise fulfilled, one step at time. Let's continue onward.

Dear Heavenly Father,

I want to receive the promises you have for my life. I open my heart to hear your voice. Please remove all distractions and false voices, so I can clearly hear you above all else. Thank you for speaking hope over my past, present and future. Help me to grow on this journey of discerning your voice and help me to overflow with hope by the power of your holy spirit. Thank you in advance for the promised land you are preparing for me. In Jesus' name, amen.

PART 2
OUR PROMISE MAKER

Carrying a promise from God

*Every Promise in Yeshua is
Yes and Amen*

OUR PROMISE MAKER

> *God is not human, that he should lie, not a human being, that he should change his mind. Does he speak and then not act? Does he promise and not fulfill?*
> **Numbers 23:19**

As we start the journey toward our prophetic promises, we must anchor ourselves in the loving nature of our Promise Maker—our beautiful King Jesus.

He is a perfect Father, a passionate Bridegroom, and a faithful Friend.

He is our Good Shepherd, our High Priest, our Great Intercessor.

He is Prince of Peace, King of Kings, and Lord of Lords.

He is Emmanuel, God with us.

He goes by many beautiful names and unique titles, each displaying his holy nature.

He is Jesus Christ, the perfect image of true love.

All for love, he gave his life on the cross for us.

That's a man we can trust.

As our perfect Leader, Jesus will lead us through every twist and turn of life, every valley and mountain. When the road gets rough, we may be tempted to doubt that his intentions toward us are truly good.

In these moments, we may feel enticed to give our ear to the voice of the accuser who taunts our promises with that age-old question, "Did God really say?"

You must stand firm in your faith.

You must ground yourself in the word of God, your anchor.

You must hold fast to your Heavenly Father's good and loving nature.

Your Promise Giver is for you. He delights in giving you the desires of your heart. He will see his promises in your life come to fruition. You can count on it.

A Father's Promise

> *And because we are his children, God has sent the Spirit of his Son into our hearts, prompting us to call out, "Abba, Father."*
> **Galatians 4:6 NLT**

I have carried many of my own prophetic promises from God. On this journey with you, I will share some that have been fulfilled, and others that are still in process.

When I was 22 years old, I was in a worship service when I heard the Holy Spirit whisper to my heart, "I am about to speak to you. The next song the worship team is about to sing has a message in it for you."

I watched as the slide changed on the old-fashioned projector, displaying all the worship lyrics on the wall at once. It was a song I had never heard before called *He is Yahweh* by Vineyard Worship. My eyes scanned the words until I found the lyrics meant for me. The song described Jesus turning all of our bitterness into sweetness. I knew Jesus was speaking to my heart.

My name, Mariel, means "bitter ocean." God had recently given me a prophetic promise about the meaning of my name. Jesus said to me, "I will turn all of the bitterness in your life into sweet. Like I healed the bitter waters of Marah in the wilderness and made them sweet[1], revealing myself as Jehovah Rapha, I will heal you."

I began to cry as I felt the presence of God touch my heart, reminding me of his promise over my identity. I then saw a vivid vision. I was getting ready in my house wearing a beautiful dress, waiting to be picked up by a date for prom.

I heard the voice of the Lord say, "Mariel, I want to be a Father to you. I want you to know me as your Provider and Protector. I want you to trust me to provide your future husband for you. I want to protect you for the right relationships I have for you. Just like a good, loving dad would be waiting by the door for a date to pick you up for prom, I want to be your Protector. Any man must go through me before they can have permission to pursue you."

As I heard the words, my heart overflowed with wonder and reassurance. My father, Francisco, passed away when I was a baby, and I had always wanted a loving dad in my life.

Could I truly know God as a good, loving Father?

At that moment, I had a choice to make. Did I want to do things my own way or allow the Lord to father me—especially in this area that was a desire of my heart?

Would I choose to accept the invitation to God's prophetic promise?

I chose to say, "Yes! I want your will for me. I want to know you as my Father. I want the promises you have for me."

It's not a journey everyone chooses to take, but I wanted God involved in my life on a deep level. I trust the intentions of my Father to write me the best love story he has for my life.

I had no clue at the time about the faith-filled adventure I was about to embark on toward my promised land. The truth is, when God is preparing a tailor-made promise for you, he will lead you through a unique process to arrive at its fulfillment.

I am now in my 30s, so waiting and long-suffering are much weightier than when I first received the promise. Time is a precious thing. It's one of the most valuable treasures we can give to God. When we choose to wait on his promise rather than make things happen in our own timing and free will, we become a sweet fragrance of worship to Jesus.

In the middle of my process, God gave several prophetic promises to me. Throughout these pages, I will share a few precious treasures of that adventure with you.

REFLECTION

> *So you have not received a spirit that makes you fearful slaves. Instead, you received God's Spirit when he adopted you as his own children. Now we call him, "Abba, Father."*
> **Romans 8:15 NLT**
>
> *If we are unfaithful, he remains faithful, for he cannot deny who he is.*
> **2 Timothy 2:13 NLT**

- Take a moment to explore three scriptures that describe God's nature. (Ex: Psalm 116:5, 1 John 4:16, Hebrews 1:3)
- Journal about three characteristics of God that you have personally experienced with a matching Bible verse.

Dear Heavenly Father,

I want to know you more deeply than ever before! Would you reveal sides of your nature and heart that I have yet to experience personally? Make my heart soft, Lord. I want to know you as not just the Keeper of my promises but the Keeper of my heart. I want to know you as a good Father. In Jesus' name, In Jesus' name, amen.

PREGNANT WITH PROMISE

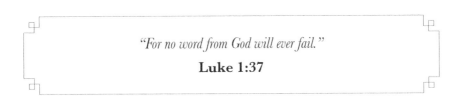

"For no word from God will ever fail."
Luke 1:37

Are you carrying an impossible promise from God?

I will let you in on a little secret. Your promise from God may seem impossible when you first receive it—because it *is* impossible.

You need a supernatural God to fulfill his word in a way only he can accomplish. You simply can't figure it out or make it happen in your own strength.

The good news is that you are now in the company of the blessed and highly favored, just like Mary. Let's take a fresh look at her story.

Enter Mary, a young teenage girl. Humble. Not a princess or a political leader or anyone of any status or notoriety. According to the world's standards, she didn't seem like the logical pick to be the mother of our Lord. Yet, God saw something in Mary that made her his handpicked choice.

In Luke 1:28, an angel appeared to her and said, "Greetings, you who are highly favored! The Lord is with you."

Mary wasn't excited when she heard the announcement—she was filled with fear!

> *So the angel told her, "Do not be afraid, Mary, for you have found favor with God. Behold, you will conceive and give birth to a son, and you are to give Him the name Jesus. He will be great and will be called the Son of the Most High. The Lord God will give Him the throne of His father David, and He will reign over the house of Jacob forever. His kingdom will never end!"*
> **Luke 1:30-33**

What did God's favor look like for Mary? She was chosen above all women to carry an impossible prophetic promise: the long-awaited Messiah, King Jesus. What a fearfully wonderful thing to be chosen by God! She was pregnant with promise.

However, this privilege came with a great cost. While God's favor held unthinkable glory, it meant she must bear the stigma of being an unwed pregnant teen. How could a virgin girl bring the Son of God into the world? Isn't that an *un*favorable way to fulfill a promise? Who would believe such a supernatural claim?

Yet, Mary was a part of fulfilling a great prophetic promise given to the prophet Isaiah, "Therefore the Lord himself will give you a sign: The virgin will conceive and give birth to a son, and will call him Immanuel" (Isaiah 7:4).

God's favor can be offensive. When God calls us to carry something significant for him, others may misunderstand and even reject what the Lord has placed within us.

Even Mary's fiancé, Joseph, struggled to believe her promise due to the unusual circumstances and debated divorcing her quietly. However, God sent an angel to Joseph in a dream to confirm the promise to him, too.

The process of a God promise can carry this kind of price tag: the loss of reputation, the stirring of offense, jealousy, or judgment in others—or even having loved ones turn their backs on you. If this happens to you, don't lose heart! You can take inspiration from Mary's simple faith and obedience.

When Mary received the angel's news, did she understand the full cost of what God had placed within her? It's uncertain. But we see a beautiful trust in Mary's response to her impossible promise:

> *"I am the Lord's servant,"* Mary answered.
> *"May your word to me be fulfilled."*
> **Luke 1:38**

May we have faith to respond to the promises of God with the same kind of wonder and childlike faith—no matter the cost. Any price we pay cannot compare to the beautiful promise God is about to bring forth in our lives.

Like Mary, God sees something special in you, too. Could it be that you are carrying an extraordinary promise from God?

Birthing a Supernatural Ministry

I had a recurring prophetic dream when I was in ministry school.

In the dreams, I was shocked to discover I was pregnant! But, like Mary, it was impossible because I was a virgin. I felt a tangible shock and fear as my mind raced: *How did this happen? I don't have a husband! Can I have this baby as a single woman? What will happen to my reputation?*

Each dream ended with the same final thought: *This must have been how Mary felt!*

Through the dreams, I felt God was giving me a symbolic message that I would "birth" something supernatural for him in my life. Like Mary, I would not only experience the favor of God but also the cost that comes with being pregnant with a God-promise.

However, there was an important puzzle piece of the dreams I was missing. I told my friend Rachel about them, and God gave her more of the interpretation.

"Mariel, God is going to call you to birth a ministry before you get married!" she said.

Her words sent chills through me. The "baby" I was carrying was a ministry. I was pregnant with a promise from God!

Honestly, her interpretation of my dreams was the last thing I wanted to hear! Getting married was one of the biggest desires of my heart, and it was my dream to start a ministry with my future husband someday. What would it look like to start a ministry as a single woman?

However, I have learned that God's timing and ways are perfect. As time passed, the meaning of the dream stood strong. I chose to actively prepare for my calling and destiny while treasuring God's prophetic promises in my heart like Mary.

REFLECTION

"Oh, how my soul praises the Lord. How my spirit rejoices in God my Savior! For he took notice of his lowly servant girl, and from now on all generations will call me blessed."
Luke 1:46-48 NLT

"Blessed is she who has believed that the Lord would fulfill his promises to her!"
Luke 1:45

Recommended Bible Reading: Luke 1:26-38

- Have you received an impossible promise from God?
- What was your first reaction to receiving the promise?
- If you need a promise from God, ask him for one! Listen for his response.

Dear Heavenly Father,

Help me to receive your prophetic promises with faith-filled wonder, like Mary. I will choose to say "Yes!" to you no matter the cost of carrying a promise. I ask for supernatural grace and courage on my way to step into everything you have planned for me. Help me bring my promises to full term for the glory of God. In Jesus' name, amen.

PROPHETIC ENCOURAGEMENT
TO THE PROMISE CARRIER

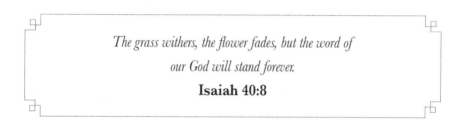

The grass withers, the flower fades, but the word of our God will stand forever.
Isaiah 40:8

I heard the Lord say:

"Dear Promise Carrier,

You are pregnant with promise. The promise inside of you is uniquely yours. You are carrying my dream for such a time as this. It's going to be tailored perfectly to your life.

Come to me, and I will show you the wonderful plans I have for you. If you need a glimpse of the promises I am preparing for you, simply spend time with me and ask me about the blessings I am speaking and singing over you. My words aren't too good to be true or wishful thinking. You are destined for the promised land.

While flowers may fade, my word will stand forever. I am with you in the beginning, middle, and end of the journey. I know the path has been long and hard, and you have wanted to give up at times, but if only you could see what I see—I see strength in you, even when you feel weak. I am proud of you for believing me for the impossible. Your faith is a sweet perfume to me.

This is not a dead-end road. This path I have set before you is leading you to your promises. But something even more significant is happening here—your pathway to your promises is leading you to me.

I have heard every single prayer. No whisper in your heart has gone unheard. I have caught every one of your tears. I treasure each one in a bottle with your name engraved on it. I keep every desire of your heart close to my heart. Every promise is yes and amen in me.

Despite how it feels, I am not slow in keeping my promise to you. My perfect timing is setting you up for the fulfillment of what I have for you. Will you trust me to lead your heart, even as I make a highway for you in the wilderness? I will make the rough places smooth and the crooked places straight so you can follow me on this narrow path.

Promise carrier, I am your Promise Keeper and Fulfiller. More than that, I want you to know me as your good, heavenly Father.

> *Every good and perfect gift is from above, coming down from the Father of the heavenly lights, who does not change like shifting shadows.* **James 1:17**

As you seek my face and follow me in obedience, you'll discover all of the custom-made blessings I have for you. Beautiful treasures await you. Delight yourself in me, and I will give you the desires of your heart."

PROPHETIC PROMISE CARRIERS

> *"Blessed are you among women, and blessed is the child you will bear! But why am I so favored, that the mother of my Lord should come to me? As soon as the sound of your greeting reached my ears, the baby in my womb leaped for joy."*
> **Luke 1:42-44**

You aren't meant to carry your prophetic promise alone, friend. God is with you, and he will send other promise carriers who will believe your story and stand with you in faith until the mountains move.

At the same time, you can expect your promise from God to be met with doubt by those who misunderstand your relationship with Jesus. That's why only a chosen, trusted few should get the privilege of knowing about your God-given treasures.

Let your heart be encouraged; God will send you unique friendships—those who will be pregnant with their own prophetic promises, too.

When Mary received her promise from God, the angel instructed her to visit her cousin, Elizabeth, who was also carrying a special word from the Lord. She was pregnant in her old age—how impossible—how supernatural!

When Mary arrived at Elizabeth's door, something incredible happened. Elizabeth felt her baby leap in her womb! One miracle recognized another miracle. Elizabeth immediately prophesied to Mary about her own baby, confirming the angel's message to Mary: In a loud voice [Elizabeth] exclaimed: "Blessed are you among women, and blessed is the child you will bear!" (Luke 1:42)

Mary could rest knowing she didn't have to explain her prophetic promise to Elizabeth—for God revealed it directly to her.

These women received a sweet, heavenly surprise: the gift of one another. They got to experience the first few months of their miraculous pregnancies together.

A Beautiful Friendship

One morning, I opened my inbox to find a surprising message waiting for me.

"I had a dream that you got engaged!" A stranger named Diana wrote. "It was a surprise party, and it happened so quickly!"

Diana's message began our Mary and Elizabeth kind of friendship. She also carried a promise from God about marriage. Not just any marriage—a God-ordained love story.

Over the next few months and years, my friend encouraged me

during the long waiting season. When others didn't understand my prophetic process, Diana understood. We talked about the challenges of hearing God about a prophetic promise, shared confirmations, prayed for one another, and reminded each other what the Lord had spoken to us.

Her friendship was an invaluable and much-needed gift to me from Jesus. We helped one another keep going on the seemingly endless road to God's promises.

Four years later, my friend and I are seeing the fulfillment of God's promises. She is engaged and will be married by the time this book is in your hands.

Jesus saw his promise through to the end. He fulfilled what he said. My own story is still unfolding.

God Will Send Your Elizabeth

God will send you Elizabeth's, too.

When carrying something supernatural from God, you must get around people who will champion and support you. Like Mary, surround yourself with other prophetic promise carriers.

Pray and expectantly look for God to send Elizabeth's to pray with, celebrate with, and believe for the miraculous together.

REFLECTION

Even Elizabeth your relative is going to have a child in her old age, and she who was said to be unable to conceive is in her sixth month. **Luke 1:36**

Do I bring to the moment of birth and not give delivery?" says the Lord.
Isaiah 66:9

Recommended Bible Reading: Luke 1:39-45

- Do you have fellow promise carriers in your life?
- If so, how have you supported one another in your promises from God?
- If you need an Elizabeth on your journey, take some time to seek the Lord and pray the prayer below.

Dear Heavenly Father,

I boldly ask you to send me others on this journey who are also carrying prophetic promises! Bring people into my life who will stand with me for the things you've spoken to me so we can support one another and celebrate together when the arrival comes. I pray you release divine appointments with my fellow promise carriers out of the blue. Thank you they are already on their way! In Jesus' name, amen.

PROTECT YOUR PROMISE

> *Whoever keeps his mouth and his tongue keeps himself out of trouble.*
> **Proverbs 21:23 ESV**

God doesn't make promises lightly. It is important to value the prophetic words he gives us while also guarding how we speak about them.

Mary and Elizabeth received similar promises from God. Their husbands, Joseph and Zechariah, also needed to receive messages from heaven about the supernatural babies their wives were carrying. Let's look at Zechariah's response.

Speechless

Zechariah waited a long time to see his promise of having a child fulfilled. So long, in fact, that he couldn't believe it when the time finally came to birth the promise.

In Luke chapter one, the angel Gabriel appeared to Zechariah in the temple to tell him that Elizabeth was miraculously pregnant. Instead of responding with faith like Mary, Zechariah immediately questioned the angel out of doubt and unbelief. Let's look at what happens in Luke 1:18-20:

Zechariah asked the angel, "How do you expect me to believe this? I'm an old man and my wife is too old to give me a child. What sign can you give me to prove this will happen?"

Then the angel said, "I am Gabriel. I stand beside God himself. He has sent me to announce to you this good news. But now, since you did not believe my words, you will be stricken silent and unable to speak until the day my words have been fulfilled at their appointed time and a child is born to you. That will be your sign!"

Gabriel caused Zechariah to become mute until John was born! By making him speechless, I believe the angel was protecting the promise while it was still vulnerable. As it says in Proverbs 18:21 (NLT), "The tongue can bring death or life; those who love to talk will reap the consequences." As the father, the words Zechariah would speak about the promise were critical to its development.

Zechariah got his voice back when John was born. The process was complete, and the promise was protected through its due date.

Zechariah Vs. Mary

Mary and Zechariah asked the angel similar questions, "How can this promise be possible?"

I believe God loves it when we ask him questions—it's part of how we deepen our friendship with him. However, are we asking to truly understand, like Mary? Or are we questioning God out of unbelief, like Zechariah?

Our heart posture matters. Let's get positioned in faith to receive the promises of God.

Speak Life

Treasure the words God speaks to you, and let faith take deep roots in your heart. Water the seeds of promise with prayers and words that bring life. A promise is vulnerable and needs shielding from negativity, doubt, and fear that may hinder its growth.

To guard your promises from negative words, it's wise to have healthy boundaries around what you share and with whom. Not everyone should get access to what God is doing in your life. Embrace wisdom and use discernment to steward what God has spoken to you.

Begin to speak words of faith and life as you protect your prophetic promises.

REFLECTION

Set a guard over my mouth, LORD; keep watch over the door of my lips.
Psalm 141:3

Finally, brothers and sisters, whatever is true, whatever is noble, whatever is right, whatever is pure, whatever is lovely, whatever is admirable—if anything is excellent or praiseworthy—think about such things.
Philippians 4:8

Recommended Bible reading: Luke 1:5-25, Luke 1:57-66

- Take a moment to reflect on how you have been thinking and speaking about the promises God has given you.
- Write down any negative thoughts and words you want to release to Jesus.
- Ask the Holy Spirit to replace the negative thoughts with words of faith and life and write them down. Pray the life-giving words over your promises!

Dear Heavenly Father,

Help me speak words of life, faith, and hope over my promises. Forgive me for any negative words I have spoken! I also choose to forgive anyone who has spoken negatively about my promises or hasn't supported me on my faith walk. I break the power of these negative words and replace them with your hopeful truth. Teach me how to protect my promises! In Jesus' name, amen.

EXPECT THE UNEXPECTED

And she gave birth to her firstborn, a son. She wrapped him in cloths and placed him in a manger, because there was no guest room available for them.
Luke 2:7

When God fulfills a promise, it often happens in a way we are not expecting. When the unexpected happens, we are invited to lean into the mystery of his ways.

Finally, after months of anticipation, the time arrived for Mary to give birth to the long-awaited prophetic promise of the Messiah.

Considering the magnitude of the miraculous event, you would think God would have made certain to reserve a room for Mary and Joseph in Bethlehem. And yet, there wasn't any space at the inn for them!

Instead, King Jesus was born in a lowly stable. I can't imagine a barn being any mother's ideal scenario to deliver a promise!

While it seemed like an imperfect beginning, the place of Yeshua's birth was a powerful prophetic sign. Church historians suggest that Jesus was born in an area of Bethlehem called Migdal Eder, which means "Tower of the Flock" in Hebrew. This is where lambs were raised by shepherds for Passover sacrifices.[1] Therefore, the setting of Jesus's birth foreshadowed his role as our Passover Lamb, the perfect sacrifice for the sins of the world.

Surrounded by glorious angels and meek shepherds, it was both a humble and miraculous beginning. The birth of Jesus was the fulfillment of Mary's prophetic promise in a way that only God could orchestrate.

Beyond Our Wildest Dreams

It's easy to build an idea—complete with blueprints, maps, and timelines—of how we expect God to fulfill his promises for us.

But in the end, the word of the Lord will be fulfilled in a way only he can accomplish. When this happens, Jesus gets all of the glory.

Sometimes, a dream, vision, or promise comes to pass exactly how we envisioned it. But so often, God only gives us a glimpse of what he has in store for us.

> *For we know in part and we prophesy in part, but when completeness comes, what is in part disappears.*
> **1 Corinthians 13:9-10**

When it comes to a prophetic promise, we may not understand the whole outcome until the appointed time for it to come to pass.

In turn, we can get disappointed when our expectations fail. We can question if God will come through for us after all.

We have to remember that it is often our own expectations—not God—that let us down. While our expectations may fail, God's true word never does. His thoughts and his ways are so much higher than our own. Perhaps God is setting you up for something far greater just around the corner.

> *Now to him who is able to do immeasurably more than all we ask or imagine, according to his power that is at work within us.*
> **Ephesians 3:20**

Our wildest imaginations cannot dream up what Jesus has in store for us. It's always so much more than we can imagine.

As we surrender our expectations, we can embrace a heart attitude of expectancy that declares, "Father, I don't know when or how you will make this promise happen, but I trust you! I believe you have a beautiful outcome for me, far better than I can ask or dream."

Like Mary, may we find our promises from God fulfilled in miraculous ways.

REFLECTION

So is my word that goes out from my mouth:
It will not return to me empty, but will accomplish what I desire and achieve the purpose for which I sent it.
Isaiah 55:11

So do not throw away your confidence; it will be richly rewarded. You need to persevere so that when you have done the will of God, you will receive what he has promised.
Hebrews 10:35-36

Recommended Bible Reading: Luke 2:1-17

- Do you have specific expectations for how God will fulfill a promise to you?
- Invite the Lord into your expectations and ask him to give you his perspective in exchange for yours.

Dear Heavenly Father,

Surprise me! I lay down my expectations of how you will fulfill my promises. Open the eyes of my heart to see how you are working in both ordinary and supernatural ways in my situation. Turn my expectations into a heart attitude of expectancy. I believe you will do more than I can ever ask or dream! In Jesus' name, amen.

MAKE ROOM FOR THE PROMISE

> *"Sing, barren woman, you who never bore a child;*
> *burst into song, shout for joy, you who were never in labor;*
> *because more are the children of the desolate woman than of her who has a husband," says the Lord.*
> *"Enlarge the place of your tent, stretch your tent curtains wide,*
> *do not hold back; lengthen your cords, strengthen your stakes.*
> *For you will spread out to the right and to the left;*
> *your descendants will dispossess nations and settle in their desolate cities."*
> **Isaiah 54:1-3**

It's hard waiting on a promise from God.

The moment we receive the word from the Lord, we may overflow with joy. However, as the weeks, months, years, and even decades pass, we can grow weary from the wait.

How do you keep hoping for a promise that God keeps speaking to you and confirming again and again, but it hasn't come to pass yet?

Imagine throwing a party before you see the promise fulfilled. It feels counterintuitive to celebrate before you see a breakthrough with your own eyes, doesn't it?

That's the kind of faith-filled action God invites Sarah into in Isaiah 54.

Like Mary and Elizabeth, Sarah carried a beautiful promise from God—she was going to become a mother. But many years have passed, and the promise looked more and more impossible.

In Isaiah 54, something unthinkable happens. God tells Sarah to rejoice while her womb is still barren. He encourages her to make room for her promise before it arrives. She needs to expand her living space because she's not just going to be a mother of one child—

She will be a mother of *many nations*.

In the middle of her barren wasteland, God speaks a more significant promise than she can comprehend.

In the same way, God encourages us to celebrate before we can see his promises come to pass in our lives. He invites us to expand our faith to make room for the new to arrive before it makes logical, practical sense.

Many times, a prophetic promise will seem impossible the moment you hear it because God is building your faith. He is calling that which is not already existing into existence. By speaking to you about that promise in advance, he is helping you get ready to receive it.

We need to make room for the promise before it comes.

God kept his promise to Sarah, and she had Isaac precisely at the time he revealed to her.

Make room. God will fulfill your promises, too.

Purple Suitcase

I was at the store when I noticed a purple carry-on in the travel section.

I don't need this, I thought to myself. *I'm not planning to travel anywhere anytime soon.*

Nonetheless, I texted a photo of it to my mom, and she said, "Get it in faith, Mariel! God is going to bring you new places."

I got the suitcase. I have come to learn that Jesus honors that kind of faith.

A few weeks later, I was on a break at work making tea in the kitchen when my boss walked in with a giant grin on her face.

"Mariel, God told me this morning that he is sending you to the nations!" She said. I was amazed that she heard the Lord on my behalf.

Shortly after that day, God called me to go on several national and international ministry trips. He also gave me the favor with my boss to take off work anytime I needed to travel for ministry. Have no doubt that I took my purple suitcase on those trips!

My purple suitcase has become a reminder of having faith for God's promises. Over the years, I have had several prophetic dreams of seeing that same purple suitcase. Through those dreams, I knew God was saying to make room for his promises before I see them.

REFLECTION

> *It was by faith that even Sarah was able to have a child, though she was barren and was too old. She believed that God would keep his promise.*
> **Hebrews 11:11 NLT**

Recommended Bible Reading: Isaiah 54, Genesis 21:1-7

Have you made room in your heart and life for God's promises? Here are some questions to reflect on.

- Ask God to show you the purpose in your current season.
- Ask him how you can make room for the promise to come.
- Write down five practical steps to get ready this week, month, and year.

Dear Heavenly Father,

Help me get my hopes up! Teach me to live with gratitude and joy now, even as I look expectantly to the future. Show me how to prepare in faith for what you are preparing for me. Then, I ask for boldness to take faith in action. Make me ready for your promise to come to pass! In Jesus' name, amen.

IN THE MIDDLE

Every year around my birthday, I ask the Lord for a prophetic word from his heart for me. It's the best gift I can think of to ask for from my Father.

My 30th birthday was coming up on February 7th, and I felt frustrated that I was still single. Yet, I waited for a word from God to give me hope for my future.

When my birthday weekend rolled around, a friend sent me a voice memo out of the blue.

"Mariel, I am on a ministry trip in Brazil, and I just met a grandmother here who has a prophetic word for you," he said. "She only speaks Portuguese, so she is going to give you the word, and a man will translate it for you."

Through a translator, the grandmother said, "The Lord is showing me a picture of a blonde girl. I have a word for her."

My friend showed her a few pictures of a few blonde women he knew, and when he got to mine, the woman responded, "Yes, that's the exact girl God is showing me."

In Portuguese, she began to give my friend a prophetic word to deliver to me, "God has her in a process. There is a beginning, middle, and end to the process. She is in the middle. God is saying he will complete the process at the right time. He has a perfect time for her promises. She hasn't known the presence of a Father in her life. He wants her to know that he is a Father to her."

Tears fell as I listened to the voice recording. Jesus reminded me that he hadn't forgotten my promise. He was still working on it.

How kind of the Lord to share a secret of my heart with a faithful grandmother in Brazil. If God can send a message to a woman in another country who speaks a foreign language, I believe he is more than capable of fulfilling the promises he gives.

This is just one of the many miraculous ways God has confirmed his word to me on my process toward my promise of a kingdom marriage—while preparing me to step into his other promises.

Hope began to fill my heart again to endure the long-suffering of the long journey. And that is the power of a prophetic promise.

God will give us a word to hold onto to keep us going, to pursue his will, and to endure the process. He has a beautiful ending planned for the story he is writing with our promises—we just have to trust him in the middle.

Trust God's Process

To every promise, there is a beginning, middle, and end.

The start of a promise is full of wonder. You are excited to see how God will bring all the beautiful details together.

The middle is where you can begin to lose heart. You may wonder if you misheard the voice of your Good Shepherd in the first place.

The promise you thought would take days is taking much, much longer.

Here, in the middle, is where the real adventure begins.

Friend, while the road may seem long and lonesome, and the mountains before you seem unconquerable, I can promise you one thing—this journey from a promise given to its fulfillment will be worth it.

It will be worth the waiting, warring, and wrestling.

Others may misunderstand your faith walk, but you are never alone.

Jesus himself is walking with you.

He is not just a Promise Maker but a Promise Fulfiller.

Even more than a Promise Fulfiller, he is a good Father.

He gets glory from our lives when he fulfills his promises to us.

He will be faithful to bring every word to pass in due time.

REFLECTION

> *It seemed like a dream, too good to be true, when GOD returned Zion's exiles. We laughed, we sang, we couldn't believe our good fortune. We were the talk of the nations—"God was wonderful to them!" GOD was wonderful to us; we are one happy people. And now, God, do it again—bring rain to our drought-stricken lives. So those who planted their crops in despair will shout "Yes!" at the harvest, So those who went off with heavy hearts will come home laughing, with armloads of blessing.*
> **Psalm 126:1-6 MSG**

- Take a moment to reflect on the promises God has given you. Write down your hopes and fears about your promise.
- Pray and give these to God! Ask him to increase your faith for the impossible.

> *Dear Heavenly Father,*
>
> *Meet me in the middle of my journey of faith on my way to your promises! Fill me with joy and strength as we go on this adventure together. I give you all my doubts, hopes, fears, and dreams. Help me, Holy Spirit! I trust you to lead me the whole way. In Jesus' name, amen.*

PROPHETIC ENCOURAGEMENT
YOUR DUE TIME IS COMING

> *Can you not discern this new day of destiny breaking forth around you? The early signs of my purposes and plans are bursting forth. The budding vines of new life are now blooming everywhere. The fragrance of their flowers whispers, "There is change in the air."*
> **Song of Songs 2:13 TPT**

I hear the Lord saying, "It's time for the barren ones to sing again! The season is changing. I am doing something new! You will be astounded at what I do. Believe before you see the breakthrough. Prepare before you see the answer. The last season's barrenness is ending, so get on track with what I am doing. Fruitfulness is coming!"

God is pruning the barrenness of hearts and lives. Where the land has been barren in your life, fruitfulness is coming. It's time to blossom. Kingdom efforts that haven't yielded results will begin to turn around. Words from the Lord that have looked dormant will come to life. The dream is not dead—it is just sleeping. It's time to wake up!

Jesus has provision for everything he does—every word and every promise he gives, he also fulfills. He will complete his work from start to finish in our lives.

Hold Fast to the Promise

> *"Do I bring to the moment of birth and not give delivery?" says the LORD.*
> **Isaiah 66:9**

When the promise seems like it will never come, and the waiting feels unbearable—you must resolve in your heart not to abort the process.

I repeat: do not abort the process! Hold fast to the promises of God. Sometimes, it feels like our promises have reached far beyond their due dates. You might not see the promise showing at first, but it begins to appear over time. Then, suddenly, it's your due date.

Ring of Fire

There may come a time when you approach the ring of fire in your process to your promises from God. During the birthing process, the "ring of fire" is a transitional moment when the baby's head crowns. The intensity of this moment may make a mother want to stop pushing.

In the ring of fire of your promise, you may want to give up. You can't—it's almost here. You must PUSH through. It's right when you feel like you can't make it another moment the baby is born. The promise finally arrives!

In your most difficult moments, you must remember that God's promises are nearer now than ever before. I am reminded of the phrase "objects in mirrors are closer than they appear" on the rearview mirror of cars. God remembers the word he spoke to you behind you in the past. Your promises are chasing you down.

> *Surely your goodness and unfailing love will pursue me all the days of my life, and I will live in the house of the LORD forever.* **Psalm 23:6 NLT**

Your due time is coming. You will make it through the birth pangs. You will persevere through the difficulty and behold the promise with your own eyes.

Treasure the Promise

When it seems like the promise is too impossible to be fulfilled, don't lose heart. Choose to treasure the words God has spoken you in your heart like Mary. When you reach the finish line, your testimony will be, "It was worth it all to carry a promise from God!"

> *But Mary treasured up all these things and pondered them in her heart.*
> **Luke 2:19**

When it seems like the promise will never be born, remember that even Sarah laughed when God told her she would have a child. Her laughter did not stop his word from coming to pass.

God's timeline may look different than yours, but if he said it, his timing will be perfect in your life. Nothing will stop it when God says, "Now!"

The answer may come at a time you don't expect. The Lord may move in a way that surprises you. That's why you must prepare for and protect your promise. Get your hopes up and prepare a celebration! Worship and praise him before the breakthrough comes.

He makes the barren wasteland bloom again.

You will bloom again.

Your promises are coming.

PART 3
WILDERNESS WONDERS

Entering the Process to the Promised Land

A sign will make you wonder

Be filled with

W o n d e r

A VISION OF A PROMISED LAND

> *But I have promised you, "You will possess their land because I will give it to you as your possession—a land flowing with milk and honey."*
> **Leviticus 20:24 NLT**

When God gives a prophetic promise, he reveals a special preview of what is yet to come. He begins to build our faith for a future brimming with hope.

When Yahweh spoke to the Israelites about inheriting the Promised Land, he painted a vision of blessing: a land flowing with milk and honey, pomegranates, figs, and grapes—a place where they would lack nothing.

His purpose behind this prophetic vision was to embolden his people, reassuring them that obedience would lead to coming blessings.

In a similar way, Jesus gives us a promise to ignite our faith for the future. He speaks to us about own promised lands, preparing us to step into destiny.

Yet, a promise given marks only the starting line of the adventure to our promised land. Like the children of Israel, we must first venture into the wilderness of wonders.

Wilderness of Wonders

> *By means of many wonders and miraculous signs, he led them out of Egypt, through the Red Sea, and through the wilderness for forty years.*
> **Acts 7:36 NLT**

Welcome to the first destination on the path to your promises, the wilderness of wonders.

It's here where we lean into the whispers and ways of Jesus.

It's here where we become more reliant on the Holy Spirit.

It's here where God prepares us for his promises.

However, that's not always our first impression. We may feel confused when the way of a promise leads us into a barren wasteland. It can appear like we are heading in the opposite direction of God's plan.

Our hearts may wonder, *Have I misheard your voice, Lord? Did I take the wrong step or disobey you to land in no-man's-land?*

While it may seem like you've somehow taken a detour, your prayers have led you here. You are exactly where you need to be. This is your separation and preparation season for your promised land.

A VISION OF A PROMISED LAND

The wilderness is where God takes his chosen ones to prepare them for destiny—just ask Moses, John the Baptist, and our Savior, Jesus Christ.

You may wonder, *Can't we bypass the wilderness, Jesus? Do we have to wander in circles when we could take a shortcut to get to our destination?*

The truth is this season is vital to your promises coming to pass and God doesn't want you to miss the wonders he has waiting here for you. The word for "wilderness" in Hebrew is *midbar* (רְבָדמ), which also means "to speak" or "to counsel."[1] The wilderness is where Jesus draws you to himself and teaches you to intimately know the sound of his voice as he directs you toward your promises.

If we could see the whole pathway at the start of the journey, we most likely would not want to take the first step. We may be intimidated by the many twists, turns, and obstacles ahead of us.

That's why a prophetic promise gives you a glimpse of the end from the beginning. God shows you a vision of the milk and honey awaiting you in your promised land across the Jordan River. He isn't doing this to tease you—he is showing you that there is purpose in the process.

Your promise is not a mirage in the desert; there is a treasure at the end of the rainbow road. Our Good Shepherd will lead us one step at a time, so we aren't overwhelmed by the path ahead.

Take heart; the wilderness is not forever.

You will possess your promises.

My 40-Day Fast

A few years ago, I was watching the opening scene of the movie *The Greatest Showman* when the Holy Spirit began to minister to me. I have a background in performing arts, and Jesus often speaks to me through creative expressions like films, plays, books, and music. The movie begins with a song called *A Million Dreams*, where the main character, played by Hugh Jackman, sings about a future full of dreams fulfilled. I started to weep as I felt Jesus encourage my heart to dream big about the beautiful plans he had for my own life.

I felt called to start a ministry to equip people in their relationship with God to bring revival to the nations. I dreamt of starting a ministry school, writing books and bible studies, running online mentorships, and releasing social media ministry to help people around the world hear God and learn how to prophesy. I had been so transformed in my own walk with Jesus through the prophetic gift that I wanted to help others encounter him, too. I also held a deep desire of my heart to get married and have a God kind of love story that would be so powerful it would shake the nations for the glory of Jesus.

Deep in my heart, I felt I needed to get more intentional about seeking Jesus for his plans for me. I sensed the Lord calling me to go on a 40-day fast to pursue his calling and promises for my life. It was the first time I had participated in a fast this long, but I felt a special grace to do it—and I did.

When my fast ended, I never felt more ready to pursue my God-given promises. I felt confident that they were right around the corner.

However, just as it appeared that my destiny doors to my promises were finally opening, the complete opposite happened. Every door slammed shut.

Wait. Wasn't my time of prayer and fasting supposed to lead me directly into God's promises for my life? I wondered. Wow was I wrong about God's timing! Instead, I started God's *process* to my promised land.

I should have known the route from fasting would lead into the wilderness. That is the biblical pattern of God's ways when leading his chosen ones into destiny. The problem was that I didn't recognize my season shift, which made me miserable for months!

Dear friend, I will tell you a valuable secret: embracing your wilderness is much better than avoiding it. You'll skip another loop around the desert if you do. Let's look at a few signs that you are in the wilderness.

7 Signs of a Wilderness Season

1. Your plans fall through, and you suddenly face shut doors on every side.
2. You find yourself stuck in the same job, location, or situation.
3. You experience constant refining in work, relationships, and other areas of life.
4. You aren't bearing fruit in your life despite all your efforts.
5. You face new obstacles and challenges that purify your faith, character, and obedience to God.
6. You keep walking around the same mountain and take the same tests on repeat with little to no breakthrough.
7. No matter how much you pray and seek God, your situation isn't changing.

The wilderness sounds like a fun process, doesn't it? Even so, you can get excited when you find yourself being led by the Holy Spirit into the desert. God is up to a great work in your life. He is preparing you for your promises.

As you follow Jesus closely on the journey ahead, you will find treasures hidden here in the wilderness of wonders waiting for you.

REFLECTION

> *He has watched over your journey through this vast wilderness. These forty years the Lord your God has been with you, and you have not lacked anything.*
> **Deuteronomy 2:7**

- **Prophetic Activation:** Are you currently in a wilderness season, or do you remember a time when you were in one? Take time to pray, ask God the following questions, and journal the response.

- "Jesus, would you show me the purpose in my wilderness season? "What areas of my life and heart are you working on?" "What lessons do you want to teach me so I can pass the tests ahead and prepare for my promises?"

Dear Lord Jesus,

I want to be ready for my promises! If the path to my promises must lead me into the wilderness, give me the grace and strength to keep following you. Help me learn every lesson and pass every test to prepare me for my promised land. Will you draw near to me and encounter me in the wilderness, Lord? I want to meet with you! Amen.

CLOUD BY DAY, FIRE BY NIGHT

> *By day the Lord went ahead of them in a pillar of cloud to guide them on their way and by night in a pillar of fire to give them light, so that they could travel by day or night.*
> **Exodus 13:21**

On this wilderness journey, we often want the whole map laid out in front of us—along with a compass, timeline, and GPS directions to guide us on our way.

While there may be times when God gives detailed instructions, he often leads us another way. He shows us one step at a time, one day at a time.

To bring the Israelites through the wilderness, God supernaturally led them by a cloud by day and a pillar of fire by night. They were never a step behind or a step ahead of him.

He kept them dependent on his leadership by providing daily direction. God wants our daily dependence, too.

If you have given Jesus your surrendered "Yes!" to the invitation to follow him no matter the cost, he will faithfully lead you forward.

Your Good Shepherd will light your path up to your promises, even if it's just enough lamp light for your next step.

The Next Right Step

> *The steps of a man are established by the Lord,*
> *when he delights in his way;*
> *though he fall, he shall not be cast headlong,*
> *for the Lord upholds his hand.*
> **Psalm 37:23-24 ESV**

Have you ever felt a holy restlessness? A deep feeling that God is leading you into something new, but you don't know what yet? You know deep down you can't stay where you are—something has to change.

Sometimes, when you don't know what to do, all you can do is take the next right step and pray for the best.

While waiting to step into one of my promises of running my own ministry, I was working at a job that made me miserable … the kind of miserable that as soon as I left work on Friday, I already dreaded the coming Monday morning.

I prayed about resigning but didn't receive a clear answer from the Lord if I should stay at my job or put in my two-week notice. At a loss, I determined it was time to leave.

The night before I planned to quit, my friend Adriana sent me a prophetic message on social media.

"God is refining and purifying you!" she said. "That's what happens in the wilderness."

While her words seemed timely, I wasn't sure how to apply them to my situation at work.

The next day, I was determined to resign. I discovered the date fell on Purim on the Hebrew calendar—the Jewish festival that celebrates the story of Esther. Like the Persian queen, I needed to have my own moment of bravery for such a time as this.

With my resignation letter in hand, I walked towards my boss's office when my coworker stopped me.

"God is purifying you!" she said. "I don't know if it is the right decision for you to quit today. Why don't you tell our overseer you are planning to resign before you tell your boss?"

I took her advice and went to my overseer's office. She invited me to sit down, and I told her my plan.

With startling confidence, she said, "You are not going to quit today. God has you on a narrow path. You don't jump off the path when it gets difficult. You need to stay the course! It's not time for you to leave yet."

I felt the weighty presence of the Holy Spirit touch me and began to cry. I knew she was prophesying the word of the Lord to me. I needed to remain in my job.

Like Esther, I boldly spoke up and gave her feedback about my job. As a result, my department was restructured, and major improvements were made to help everyone on my team. The atmosphere of my workplace shifted, and I could finally enjoy work.

God used the situation to increase my boldness and leadership—and even bring others into their own breakthroughs, too! Like my friend and co-worker prophesied, he was purifying me to prepare me for my calling to ministry. Although I didn't receive a specific word from the Lord about what action to take, my prayerful decision to take the next right step accelerated my destiny.

It can be difficult to discern God's voice in life—especially when it comes to major life decisions like taking or leaving a job, moving to a new city, or getting married. God will give us better guidance than a GPS—but sometimes, we must get our car in motion first. He will redirect us to get back on track if we take a wrong turn.

We need to prayerfully move forward and trust him to make our paths straight. He will be our cloud by day and fire by night, leading us one step at a time.

REFLECTION

> *He restores my soul. He leads me in paths of righteousness for his name's sake.*
> **Psalm 23:3 ESV**

- Have you ever felt stuck in a challenging situation? Did you stay put or take a leap of faith?

- If you currently feel stuck, weigh the pros and cons of making a change.

- Ask God, "What is my next best step?"

Dear Lord Jesus,

Lead me in the best way I should go! Guide me along the right paths for your namesake (Psalm 23). I pray for courage to take the next best steps, trusting you will catch me if I stumble and redirect me if I get off course. Thank you for adding momentum to my life as I step out in faith. Amen.

MIRACLE MANNA

> *Then the LORD said to Moses, "I will rain down bread from heaven for you. The people are to go out each day and gather enough for that day. In this way I will test them and see whether they will follow my instructions."*
> **Exodus 16:4**

One of the most incredible ways God speaks throughout the Bible—and still speaks through today—is through signs and wonders.

The Hebrew word for "sign" is *owth* (אוֹת), meaning "a flag, beacon, monument, evidence, mark, miracle, or token."[2] It implies the supernatural evidence of God's presence and activity in our lives.

A "wonder" in Hebrew is the word *pele*, which expresses God's astonishing and hard-to-understand acts.[3] They say a sign will make you wonder. I have found this to be true.

What is it?

God provided food for the children of Israel in the wilderness through a supernatural sign: bread from heaven.

Each morning, they would wake up to find the ground freshly covered in mysterious white food. This miracle manna—along with quail—helped them endure the wilderness testing one day at a time.

When God leads us into the wilderness, he will sustain us with what we need to keep going, too.

In the Hebrew language, the word *manna* (מן) means "What is it?"[4]

An unusual sign will inspire us to ask God, "What is it? What does it mean?"

When a sign has you asking these questions, you are invited into a holy conversation with Jesus. He wants to reveal something new and important to you.

5 Examples of Signs with Confirmations

While there are many ways that God may speak to us, here are a few practical examples of signs with accompanying confirmations.

1. You see the same Bible verse multiple times in a week, confirming the work God is doing in your life.
2. You hear the still, small voice of the Holy Spirit speak a word to you, and then events in life play out in such a way to confirm his word.
3. You see a specific symbol—such as a butterfly, bird, phrase, or number—on repeat that gets your attention and causes you to seek Jesus for the deeper meaning.

4. You have a dream or vision, and then it unfolds in your waking life, giving you wisdom and insight.

5. You pray for guidance, and then someone coincidentally speaks a word of wisdom that aligns with what you have been praying about.

3 Parts to Understanding Prophetic Signs

There are three steps to understanding a prophetic sign or wonder from God.

1. Receive revelation: Revelation is what God reveals, whether it be a prophetic sign, wonder, word, vision, or dream. It is not the meaning—simply the experience.

2. Learn the interpretation: Explore the meaning of the prophetic revelation through prayer, searching the Bible, and practical research. Write down what God reveals to you about the interpretation.

3. Discover the application: How can you practically apply the interpretation of the revelation? Is there an action step God is calling you to take or is it a call to prayer?

Learning to Love

Let me share a practical example of this prophetic process with you in understanding a sign from God. I kept seeing the same Bible verse several times in a month: "A friend loves at all times. Proverbs 17:17." I knew God was speaking to me and giving me prophetic revelation, but I didn't know what it meant or how it applied to my life.

As I sought Jesus for the interpretation, he told me he was teaching me the importance of being a "friend that loves at all times." He wanted me to learn to love others unconditionally and with action, no matter their response. This is the way of Jesus—he is the friend that loves at all times.

After I discovered the interpretation, I applied it to my life. I intentionally showed the unconditional love of Jesus to those God brought in my path—especially those more difficult to love. In fact, I believe God was refining my character by asking me to show love-in-action to those who hurt and rejected me.

One more step is to test the fruit of the prophetic process. In my case, the prophetic revelation brought me closer to Jesus and to his people. God was teaching me how to love others more deeply. His work in my life aligned with the written Word. Those are signs of good fruit. However, if we bear negative fruit, we will need to bring the revelation, interpretation, and application to God again in prayer and ask for his discernment—and dismiss anything rotten.

Throughout this journey, we will talk more about testing prophetic promises from God and how to grow even deeper in discerning his voice and leading.

Keep Seeking

When God gives us personal and prophetic signs and wonders, we are often left wondering, "What is it? What does it mean?" So many people stop at this question and don't continue to seek the Lord for the deeper meaning. When it comes to understanding what God is saying, bring everything to him in prayer and seek the scriptures for the interpretation. Keep asking God to reveal to you what your "manna" means, and he will show you how it applies to your life.

God will give you daily bread to demonstrate his leadership and provision in your life. He will use his signs to point the way forward to the promised land.

REFLECTION

> *The people of Israel called the bread manna. It was white like coriander seed and tasted like wafers made with honey.*
> **Exodus 16:31**
>
> *He humbled you, causing you to hunger and then feeding you with manna, which neither you nor your ancestors had known, to teach you that man does not live on bread alone but on every word that comes from the mouth of the LORD.*
> **Deuteronomy 8:3**

Prophetic Activation: Do you have manna from God that has prompted you to ask, "What is it? What does this mean?"

- Take time to search the scriptures for a biblical and practical meaning of the sign.
- Ask God, "Will you give me understanding and revelation about the meaning of this sign? Why are you showing me this?" Listen for the voice of the Holy Spirit and journal his response.

> *Dear Lord Jesus,*
>
> *I ask for daily fresh manna to sustain me and keep me moving forward until we reach the promises you have for me. Please give me a spirit of wisdom and revelation to better understand the signs you are showing me. Thank you for providing for me in the wilderness! Amen.*

OUR BREAD OF LIFE

> *"I am the bread of life. Your ancestors ate the manna in the wilderness, yet they died. But here is the bread that comes down from heaven, which anyone may eat and not die. I am the living bread that came down from heaven."*
> **John 6:48-51**

Jesus is the ultimate sign and wonder.

In John 6, after he miraculously multiplied the fish and loaves to feed the crowds, they searched for him. Jesus addressed the heart of their pursuit:

"Very truly I tell you, you are looking for me, not because you saw the signs I performed but because you ate the loaves and had your fill. Do not work for food that spoils, but for food that endures to eternal life, which the Son of Man will give you." John 6:26-27

They experienced a miraculous sign, but now they sought him for a free meal. Yet, their deeper hunger was spiritual; they longed for Jesus himself. He tells the crowds he is the Bread of Life, the Manna that came down from heaven (John 6:35).

Every sign, every wonder points us to our Living Bread, Jesus Christ. He is the one who satisfies us with what we need through life's wilderness.

Seek Him First

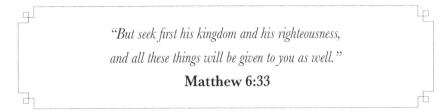

"But seek first his kingdom and his righteousness, and all these things will be given to you as well."
Matthew 6:33

The goal on this journey isn't simply to seek a sign but to seek the One who gives the sign.

Jesus paid a high price on the cross to restore connection with us; he gave his life all because of his great love for us. He has given us the beautiful gift of an intimate relationship with him—and relationships involve communication. One of the ways he will speak with us is through the language of signs and wonders.

Though some may question the appropriateness of seeking signs and confirmations from God, I believe Jesus delights in guiding us in the right direction. It honors him when we seek his help. In Proverbs 3:5-6, we are invited to pursue God's direction in all areas of life: "Trust in the Lord with all your heart and lean not on your own understanding; in all your ways submit to him, and he will make your paths straight."

With this idea in mind, seeking a sign is all about the position of our hearts.

Heart Matters

Jesus performed outstanding miracles, yet many still did not believe his words. He rebuked the religious leaders when they demanded a sign (Matt. 16:4) because they asked out of doubt, unbelief, and offense. They sought to disprove his ministry and punish him. Their hardened hearts burst with the wrong motives.

However, if our intention is to seek Jesus to deepen our relationship with him, we belong to a different category—God's family. We are a royal sons or daughters of Jesus Christ with the access to seek our heavenly Father's face and discover his kingdom.

Furthermore, in the Lord's prayer (Matt. 6:11), we are invited to pray, "Give us today our daily bread."

Did you catch that? Jesus delights to give you "daily" bread of his presence. We are invited to a spiritual pursuit, where we can partake of his words of life daily.

On this adventure to our promises, it's important to remember that he is the One our hearts truly seek. As we pursue him first from a pure motive to know him, signs and wonders may follow.

REFLECTION

Then Jesus declared, "I am the bread of life. Whoever comes to me will never go hungry, and whoever believes in me will never be thirsty."
John 6:35

"Do not be afraid, little flock, for your Father has been pleased to give you the kingdom."
Luke 12:32

Recommended Bible Reading: John 6

- Can you remember a moment when God sustained you by speaking a word to you? What did he give you as your "daily bread"?

Dear Lord Jesus,

I want to seek you first in every area of my life! I come to you thirsty and hungry. Thank you for being the Bread of Life that sustains me. I ask for your daily bread to keep me going through the hills and valleys of my path to your promises. Please satisfy my soul in a way only you can. Amen.

SIGN LANGUAGE

> *"People of Israel, listen! God publicly endorsed Jesus the Nazarene by doing powerful miracles, wonders, and signs through him, as you well know."*
> **Acts 2:22 NLT**

I like to compare signs from God to road signs on the highway.

I am from Georgia, so I often drive through Atlanta. The further north I travel through the city, the more frequent the signs become for Tennessee and South Carolina. The signs become even more frequent the closer I get to my destination.

On the other hand, if I were to drive down the wrong side of the highway, I would begin to see signs that say, "WRONG WAY! TURN AROUND!"

In the same way, God may be getting our attention with his signs.

Signs show where Jesus is at work in our lives to encourage us, move us forward, get us unstuck, stay on the path, warn us, or give us wisdom. The more frequently the signs become in our lives, the more the Lord may be showing us that we are heading in the right direction and getting closer to our destination—or we need to turn around and take a new route.

If we rely on technology like GPS to get us where we need to go, how much more can we depend on our heavenly Father to guide us?

Build History with Jesus

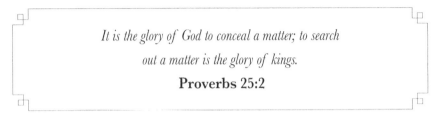

It is the glory of God to conceal a matter; to search out a matter is the glory of kings.
Proverbs 25:2

If a sign inspires you to pursue Jesus wholeheartedly, I would argue that experience bears good fruit in your life. What a beautiful thing!

People often come to me for insight into the supernatural signs they have experienced. While I am honored that they trust me with their prophetic experiences, I want to teach them how to seek Jesus for the answer with all their heart, mind, soul, and strength.

I want to remind them of their valuable opportunity to go on a treasure hunt with God. That's where we build a personal history with him. That's how we learn to discern the Good Shepherd's voice. That's where we get fueled with the oil of intimacy that keeps us burning for Jesus.

If God is showing you the sign, he wants to speak to you directly about it. It's a personal message just for you. A sign will lead you into a beautiful hide-n-seek adventure with your heavenly Father. And those who seek God find him, even if it takes a little time.

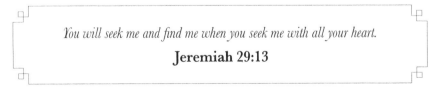

You will seek me and find me when you seek me with all your heart.
Jeremiah 29:13

With that said, I want to share a few supernatural signs God gave me in my wilderness journey.

REFLECTION

Set up road signs; put up guideposts. Take note of the highway, the road that you take. Return, Virgin Israel, return to your towns.
Jeremiah 31:21

Whether you turn to the right or to the left, your ears will hear a voice behind you, saying, "This is the way; walk in it."
Isaiah 30:21

- Do you remember a time when God sent you a sign to show you were moving in the right direction?
- Has God given you a sign to warn you or tell you to change direction? How did you respond?

Dear Lord Jesus,

I desire to follow you with my whole heart and life! As I call to you, I open my heart to how you may respond. Will you release signs and wonders to guide me on the right paths? Please give me discernment to know when a sign is from you, along with the interpretation to understand what it means. I want to seek you and find you. Amen.

THE SIGN OF THE PRAYING MANTIS

September 8, 2018

I have experienced a handful of supernatural encounters with God that have marked me forever. How God chose a bug, of all things, to give me a message is one for the books. Let me share my story with you.

My 40-day fast ended around Rosh Hashanah, the Jewish New Year. It felt significant that I was entering into a new year and a new beginning at this time. As I shared earlier, I was hopeful that my promises were so close.

On the morning of the first day of Rosh Hashanah, I headed toward my car to go to work. As I reached for the car door handle, I jumped back with a start.

I looked down to find a giant, white praying mantis staring back at me, blocking me from getting into my car. I couldn't miss it. I felt a wave of the Holy Spirit. I was filled with wonder.

THE SIGN OF THE PRAYING MANTIS

It was a sign! *But what did it mean?*

My roommate, Katherine, came over, and we observed the praying mantis together. *How odd!*

The wonder of the sign stayed with me all day. Later that night, Katherine called me onto our front porch, "Mariel, you have to see this! There are two more praying mantises out here!"

I came outside and looked up. There were two green praying mantises next to our porch light.

"What do you think this means?" I asked. "Is there something I am supposed to do?"

"Well, we could worship the Lord!" she said.

So, we did. I got my guitar, and we worshiped Jesus and prayed together. Filled with wonder like Mary, I pondered those treasures, those strange signs, as we worshiped the Lord.

It was a "manna" moment. *What did it mean? What was God saying?*

I learned that the word *mantis* is a Greek word that means "seer, prophet."[5] *Therefore,* praying *mantis* means praying *prophet.*

Through this unusual sign, I felt God tell me to pray and prophesy my promises from him. I needed to partner in faith for what he wanted to do in my life, and not wait passively for them to happen.

Such is our responsibility on the path to a prophetic promise: we pray the word the Lord gave us, and we prophesy his promise until we see the breakthrough come.

As the weeks passed, I occasionally looked around my porch for more praying mantis visitors.

One day, the Holy Spirit told me, "You will not see a praying mantis randomly or when you are looking for it. Every time you see the praying mantis, it will be a sign to you."

The praying mantis was the first of many supernatural signs and wonders that would follow. On the journey through the wilderness of wonders, I would be like a praying mantis—a praying prophet—interceding for God's will to be done and prophesying it until I saw the promise with my own eyes.

Return of the Praying Prophet

September 9, 2019

One year later, I was driving home from Atlanta from a friend's bridal shower. I overcame my introverted tendencies to spend the afternoon with a room of mainly strangers to celebrate one of my best friends from high school before her November wedding. I was glad that I did. I made new friends over teatime of clotted cream, scones, and talk of Manhattan and Broadway.

As I made the straight-shot home that Sunday night, I began to pour out my honest thoughts to God. It's a long drive, so there's plenty of time to think. It was a year to the day that I saw the first praying mantis.

Jesus, it's been a whole year. I love your signs. I love all of the wonders. I love the way you speak to me. More than a sign, I want my situation to turn around. Will my promises ever come true, or do I need to let them go?

Twenty minutes outside of town, I realized the date was September 9th. That would make the date 9/9/2019. Nine, nine, nine. I saw a license plate in front of me with the number 999.

THE SIGN OF THE PRAYING MANTIS

Sometimes, God uses numbers to catch my attention and to speak a prophetic message to me, and he often points me to Bible verses to explain what he is saying.

I began to think aloud to myself. *The number nine often represents finality in the Bible. It is a picture of God judging fruit.*[6] *There are nine fruits of the Holy Spirit mentioned in Galatians 5. The Father comes to judge the fruit in our lives, whether good or bad. Then, he prunes it or lets it keep growing, as Jesus talks about in John 15. Nine, nine, nine. A sign, a sign, a sign. What could it mean? Is God judging my process? Am I bearing good fruit?*

I arrived home close to midnight, exhausted. As I was getting ready to sleep, I realized I left something important in my car, so I reluctantly went to get it. I walked outside and turned on my porch light. That's when I saw it.

It was a praying mantis!

I looked up just in time to see it crawl from the roof onto the porch ceiling above me. I couldn't believe my eyes.

"Katherine! Come here!" I screamed for my roommate. "It's a praying mantis!"

She came out on the porch, and we looked up at the bug together. Almost exactly one year ago, we stood in the same spot, looking at two praying mantises on the ceiling. I hadn't seen one since. A sign will make you wonder.

I searched for the praying mantis photos from the year before to double-check the date. I used a website to enter the current date (9/9/2019) and the previous one (9/8/2018) to see how much time had passed. The days were close to exactly 365 plus a few hours apart.

Yes, I know it's an insect, but God will even use his creation to speak to us! I couldn't help but think that this was how the Lord was telling me to keep prophesying and praying for my promises.

Through the date 9/09/2019 and the number 999, I felt God was saying that he was judging the fruit of my prophetic process and ruled it as good. I was drawing closer to Jesus through my journey; he would not "prune it" and bring it to an end. My process to my promised land was going to continue.

The praying mantis returning was my sign that God was not finished with my promises.

Supernatural Confirmations

> *Then the disciples went out and preached everywhere, and the Lord worked with them and confirmed his word by the signs that accompanied it.*
> **Mark 16:20**

When God continually repeats a supernatural sign, like a praying mantis, it's time to pay attention. He is likely confirming his word to you. You are invited to deeper conversation with Jesus.

The word "confirm" means to make firm or firmer, to add strength to, or to establish.[7] Confirmations from God may come in the form of timely scripture, signs, dreams, visions, prophetic words, divine coincidences, and supernatural encounters. God may surprise you with how he confirms his word to you.

While some may chalk up these experiences up to mere coincidence, perhaps Jesus is doing a special work. He is establishing his word to you and strengthening your faith for his prophetic promises in your life.

REFLECTION

> *And now, O LORD God, I am your servant; do as you have promised concerning me and my family. Confirm it as a promise that will last forever.*
> **2 Samuel 7:25 NLT**
>
> *Confirm to your servant your promise, that you may be feared.*
> **Psalm 119:38 ESV**

- Have you noticed God giving you a supernatural sign on repeat?
- How has Jesus confirmed his word to you about your promises?

> *Dear Lord Jesus,*
>
> *Release supernatural confirmation of your promises! Help me to recognize when you are putting a sign on repeat in my life. Thank you for establishing your word and strengthening my faith! I pray each confirmation will draw me closer to your heart. Amen.*

THE SIGN OF THE CARDINAL

*He who was seated on the throne said,
"I am making everything new!"*
Revelation 21:5

A few weeks after the return of the praying mantis, I decided to spend my lunch break seeking Jesus. I walked from my office to a smoothie place and opened my journal to write.

I heard the Holy Spirit say something unexpected, "Look to the sign of the cardinal."

I stopped writing. *The sign of the cardinal? What does that mean?*

I remembered a dream I had of a red cardinal bird a few months earlier. A cardinal landed on my shoulder. Uncharacteristic of a bird prone to the freedom of the skies, it remained there, unafraid. The dream puzzled me. Like Mary, I treasured it in my heart. I began to see cardinals all of the time when I would pray in a garden in my city.

God's still, small voice continued, "I can make all things new. I can resurrect any promise from the grave. A cardinal is red, like the color of the blood of Jesus. This is a reminder of my resurrection power. Sometimes, you must let a bird, a promise, fly away—even die—for a season. I can always bring it back to life. Nothing is impossible for me."

I looked at the clock and realized it was time to go. I pondered the words as I headed back to the office.

As I passed by a couple having lunch outside, their little boy stood on his chair and shouted, "IT'S A PRAYING MANTIS!"

A praying mantis had fallen from the tree above him and landed on his shoulder. He shook it off, and it was now on the path before me. I bent down and took a picture with my phone.

This is so unusual, I thought to myself. I remembered that a praying mantis means "praying prophet"—it can symbolize one who prays and prophesies God's promises.

It felt like a prophetic moment, and it seemed like that little boy was unintentionally calling me a praying prophet.

As I walked away, I heard the Lord say, "Keep praying until you see your promise transformed."

When I returned to my desk, the Lord said, "Ask your co-worker if she knows the prophetic meaning of the praying mantis."

I worked for a ministry, and my co-worker was highly prophetic. She was passing by my desk, so I asked her.

"I don't know about praying mantises," she said. She paused, looking at me for a moment in deep thought. Then she continued, "But God wants me to tell you about cardinals."

I began to tear up, shocked. "God just spoke to me about the sign of the cardinal."

"Cardinals are a special sign to me," she said. "Every time I see one, God is getting my attention. If he is showing you the cardinal, ask the Lord how to posture yourself in faith. Stand your ground in prayer."

I couldn't believe what I was hearing. I knew that God was speaking to me through her. He confirmed his sign and invited me to seek him for the deeper meaning. It was time to keep asking the Lord, "What is it? What does it mean?"

Answered Prayer

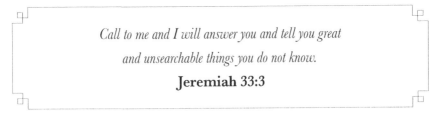

Call to me and I will answer you and tell you great and unsearchable things you do not know.
Jeremiah 33:3

When God speaks a mystery to us, it may take time to unravel the true meaning. It's like putting a giant jigsaw puzzle together, piece by piece.

We can look at the cover of the puzzle on the box and see what we are trying to create. But staring at a thousand jumbled pieces can be confusing and overwhelming.

How will all of these pieces fit together? It takes time and dedication to find out.

After two years of trying to put the puzzle pieces together, God gave me a dream about the meaning of the cardinal.

In the dream, I saw my promises begin to take place. God was preparing all of the details like a surprise party. I saw a painting of a red cardinal on my wall. Suddenly, it came to life! The bird grew huge—as large as a human!

As I saw the cardinal come to life, I had a clear revelation in the dream. After years of seeing the cardinal sign, the Lord said it meant to me "ANSWERED PRAYER."

Although the meaning is much deeper and personal to me, the general meaning of the cardinal sign is that "God answers my prayers!"

As this happened in the dream, a man named Jim approached me and said, "Tell us about the sign of the cardinal!"

"You can read about it in my book," I responded.

"Oh, you don't need to put that in the book," he said slyly. I sensed that he was trying to stop God's promises from coming to pass just as they were emerging.

The name *Jim* is derived from the Hebrew name *Jacob*, which means "supplanter, deceiver."[8] I knew I was not supposed to listen to nor obey the voice of the deceiver.

"The book is already written!" I said with an authoritative finality and walked away. My response was a sign I had passed an important test. Through my journey, I learned to protect my prophetic promises and lean only on the voice of the Lord.

The sign of the cardinal gave me the strength to keep praying for my promises until the answer came. This book in your hands is the fulfillment of one of my prophetic promises; this is one of my answered prayers.

In the coming pages, I will share even more prophetic insight into both the meaning of the cardinal and praying mantis to encourage you in your own walk with Jesus.

Our Great Intercessor

God sends signs to let us know he hears us when we call to him. He's working on the answer.

When we grow tired and weary of praying for the breakthrough, we can take inspiration from our great high priest, Jesus Christ, who sits at the right hand of the throne of God and lives to make intercession for us.

> *Because Jesus lives forever, he has a permanent priesthood. Therefore he is able to completely save those who come to God through him, because he always lives to intercede for them.*
> **Hebrews 7:24-25**

When the weeks, months, and years seem to pass without a breakthrough, be filled with new hope today. Jesus hushes all of heaven to hear you when you call—he will answer you (Jer. 33:3). He will hand you the final puzzle pieces you need to complete the picture.

The praying mantis is the sign to keep praying and prophesy God's promises and will to be done on earth as it is in heaven. The cardinal is a sign that your prayers matter and the answer is coming. Don't stop praying from a place of faith and belief. Your God is the God who answers prayer. Your answer is on the way.

REFLECTION

> *You who answer prayer, to you all people will come.*
> **Psalm 65:2**
>
> *Rejoice always, pray continually, give thanks in all circumstances; for this is God's will for you in Christ Jesus.*
> **1 Thessalonians 16-18**

- Do you remember a time when God answered your prayers? Make a list of 5-10 answered prayers from the last few years.

- Take time to give God thanks for all he has already accomplished!

- Write down your new prayer requests and thank God for the coming answered prayers.

Dear Lord Jesus,

Thank you for answering my prayers! You have been so faithful to me, Jesus. While I await more answers to my requests and petitions yet to be fulfilled, strengthen my faith with your confirmations. Teach me to pray without ceasing. Continue to deepen our friendship on this holy treasure hunt adventure. I praise you in advance for the answered prayers on the way! Amen.

MY HIDDEN MANNA

> *Whoever has ears, let them hear what the Spirit says to the churches. To the one who is victorious, I will give some of the hidden manna.*
> **Revelation 2:17**

During my own wilderness journey, slowly, surely, I began to discover the hidden manna God left for me to find—the beautiful signs and wonders of his presence.

Through dreams and visions, cardinals and rhema wards, praying mantises and unusual coincidences, and many other road signs, I entered a holy conversation with Jesus.

I continually asked, *"God, what does this mean? What are you saying through these signs?"*

And he began to answer me, one step, one sign at a time. He gave me daily bread and sustained me with his words of life.

The wilderness has been challenging, but can I tell you? I wouldn't exchange my manna for anything in the world; I wouldn't trade it to shortcut my process and get to my promised land sooner.

The signs and wonders Jesus gave me are a kind of treasure that no amount of money can ever buy. There is no cafe in the history of the world that you can walk up to and order an encounter with God. You can only receive this kind of invaluable gift through seeking Jesus in the secret place of his presence.

My hidden manna, representing my history with God, is completely priceless. It's more precious than gold or silver to me.

We find our hidden manna in all of the big and little ways he builds an intimate relationship with us on the journey.

He hides so we can find him.

And find him, we will—if we seek him and don't give up.

Lean On Your Beloved

> *Who is this coming up from the wilderness leaning on her beloved?*
> **Song of Songs 8:5**

Your wilderness of separation is meant to be a place of preparation. God has not set you *aside*—he has set you *apart* for a great purpose.

Jesus is not solely focused on getting you to your land flowing with milk and honey, he is teaching you to lean on him.

By the gentle way he leads you, he is showing you how to yield to the ways of his Spirit. Through finding him in his signs and wonders, he is making you sensitive to his voice. By giving you daily bread, he is building a friendship with you.

Reflecting on my own desert season, I see how Jesus connected the dots in my life. I see the painful, necessary preparation, stretching, and growing—all of it—held a specific purpose. The Father was molding me like the clay on the potter's wheel. He was teaching me to overcome. He was making me ready for my promises and my calling.

The wilderness is where I learned to lean on Jesus. It is where Yeshua drew me close to him in a deeper, more-than-dictionaries-can-describe kind of way.

The wilderness leads us into his will, not away from it. Even when the road gets rough and we don't think we can take another step forward, God will give us supernatural grace to press on until we see the promised land. In this desert journey, God is preparing you for your prophetic promises.

In the coming chapters, we will explore more aspects of God's preparation season—his appointed timing, the battlefield of faith, and the refiner's fire—as we head toward the promised land.

When his work is complete, you will come out of the wilderness season leaning on Jesus, moving in power and love. Your life and testimony will become a sign to others of the miraculous power of a promise-keeping God.

REFLECTION

> *It is the glory of God to conceal things, but the glory of kings is to search things out.*
> **Proverbs 25:2 ESV**
>
> *A voice of one calling: "In the wilderness prepare the way for the LORD; make straight in the desert a highway for our God."*
> **Isaiah 40:3**

Take a moment to reflect on your journey to your promises so far.

- How has God encouraged you to keep going on the wilderness road?
- How has he protected you and provided for you?
- What Bible verses, worship songs, and messages have ministered to your heart on the journey?
- What hidden treasures of "manna" have you found in your wilderness?

Dear Lord Jesus,

I want to come out of the wilderness leaning on you! Teach me to rely more and more on you every day. Help me find all of the hidden manna, the signs, wonders, and miracles you have prepared on my path! I don't want to miss anything you have to say to me or show me! I pray to enjoy my wilderness journey to the fullest because you are right here with me. Amen.

PROPHETIC ENCOURAGEMENT
WONDER UPON WONDER

> *Therefore once more I will astound these people with wonder upon wonder;*
> *the wisdom of the wise will perish, the intelligence of the intelligent will vanish.*
> **Isaiah 29:14**

I hear the Lord saying, "Come to me, and I will astound you with wonder upon wonder again. Seek me, and I will guide you one step with my language of love tailored to you. Like children with a secret code language with their friends, I want to speak to you in a language all our own. I want to show you beautiful things, wonderful things written in my written word and woven into the fabric of your everyday life. I want to show you my signs and wonders—my love notes—all around you.

When you call, I will answer you. I will embolden you again on this pathway to your promises. When you feel most weary, I will release new waves of wonders to revive your heart again. Watch for surprising signs that will make you wonder and draw you closer to me in pursuing their meaning.

I have fresh manna for you today. I don't want you to live off yesterday's revelation! Like the Israelites found new manna every morning, I have fresh words and wonders for you daily. Come to my table and eat until you are full!

Your wilderness time is perfecting my work in you. This season will not last forever—it will end soon, and a new day will break; a season of fruit is on the horizon.

But here in the middle, I am after your heart. Let my love for you overwhelm you! Even now, I am washing away your disappointment and discouragement. I am replacing the weariness of the journey with joyful expectations of good things to come. I am turning your valley of trouble into a door of hope—a new door that can only open at the sound of my voice.

> *Therefore I am now going to allure her; I will lead her into the wilderness and speak tenderly to her. I will return her vineyards to her and transform the Valley of Trouble into a gateway of hope.*
> **Hosea 2:4-5 NLT**

Will you give me all your questions, doubts, and fears? They aren't too heavy for me; I will bear them for you. I will turn your worry into wonder again. "Therefore do not worry about tomorrow, for tomorrow will worry about itself. Each day has enough trouble of its own" (Matthew 6:34).

I am anointing your head with fresh oil of joy. I am baptizing you with wild wonder to make it through the mystery of the journey I have you on. I am taking care of you. Your story is not over. There is so much more I have for you. Will you lean on me, my beloved?

> *"Remember not the former things, nor consider the things of old. Behold, I am doing a new thing; now it springs forth, do you not perceive it? I will make a way in the wilderness and rivers in the desert."*
> **Isaiah 43:19 ESV**

I am doing a new thing in your life, so forget the pain of the past! Do not look back like Lot's wife but move confidently ahead. I am making a way in your wilderness. My Holy Spirit is guiding you like streams in the desert season.

As the journey continues, you will see my hidden hand embroidering the plans I have for you, one stitch at a time, to reveal a beautiful design.

As you expectantly wait and watch for the new thing I am doing in your life, only one thing is now needed of you: spend time in my presence. I will take care of the rest."

PART 4
JUST IN TIME

*Embracing the Mystery of God's Perfect
Timing on the Path to Your Promise*

GOD'S PERFECT TIMING

> *"At the right time, I, the Lord, will make it happen."*
> **Isaiah 60:22 GW**

It often seems like God moves at two speeds in our lives:

- Really slow; and
- Really fast

His timing is a mystery. While we long to see God move quickly, there is so much purpose in the slow seasons.

Maybe it is not that God isn't answering your prayers. He's rearranging things to prepare you for the very promises you are praying for. If only you saw how he is positioning your life like pieces on a chess board—in such a strategic, calculated way—to declare a final "checkmate!" with a perfectly timed winning move.

There will be a grace for things to come together — and quickly in his timing.

Perhaps in the waiting, God is protecting you from what you cannot see. I think we would be very humbled to glimpse the complete picture of our lives as God does. We would witness all of the times he stepped in on our behalf and saved us from something we thought we wanted. An opportunity, door, connection, or desire may look good on the surface, but our good Father sees through it all—he discerns the hidden motives of the heart and knows the outcome of every situation.

When we submit our will and way to him, he will block any wrong person, place, or thing to protect us. At the same time, he is keeping us for all of the beautiful blessings he has in store. We can truly trust him to be outstanding at his job of being a good Father.

So, trust the slowness of the desert season if God has placed you there. He is preparing you, along with what you are praying for. He cares more about the promises, desires, and cares of your heart than you can imagine.

He has an expiration date on your waiting season.

The countdown is on.

The timer is set to go off.

And then suddenly, when the fullness of God's divine timing finally arrives, there will be no more time to wait!

You must leave the wilderness and head into the promised land.

Believe it or not, you may not always feel ready when it's God's time—even if you have waited a long time for it.

So, lean into your wilderness waiting as you lean on Jesus. Maybe that's exactly where he wants you.

Surprise Party

> *May the God of hope fill you with all joy and peace as you trust in him, so that you may overflow with hope by the power of the Holy Spirit.*
> **Romans 15:13**

In my own journey to my prophetic promises, despair has tried to set in more times than I can recount. However, a small but pivotal moment shifted my heart towards hope in the waiting.

While at a writer's retreat in Moravian Falls, North Carolina, I asked a friend to pray for me. She gave me a piece of advice I'll never forget.

"When you can't see what God is doing in your situation, imagine Jesus preparing a surprise party for you behind the scenes," she said. "He is getting every detail ready for your arrival to surprise you at just the right time. He wants you to know he is preparing something beautiful for you while you wait on him."

Her words were a healing balm to my heart. Instead of feeling forgotten by the Lord, a renewed sense of hope ignited within me. What if God is taking elaborate care in planning the answer to my prayers?

Can it be that wild to believe Jesus is *that* kind? I believe he is.

God is up to something in your life, even when you can't see him working. He has not forgotten you. Our kind King, Jesus Christ, is the God of all hope, and he is preparing surprises for you at just the right time.

Let hope fill your heart as you imagine the day you hear the Lord say, "Surprise!"

REFLECTION

He has made everything beautiful in its time. He has also set eternity in the human heart; yet no one can fathom what God has done from beginning to end.
Ecclesiastes 3:11

For in this hope we were saved. But hope that is seen is no hope at all. Who hopes for what they already have? But if we hope for what we do not yet have, we wait for it patiently.
Romans 8:24-25

- When was the last time you experienced a good surprise? What happened, and how did you feel?
- Review a few scriptural promises for those who wait on the Lord. (Isaiah 30:18, Lamentations 3:25, Isaiah 64:4, Psalm 37:34, Isaiah 40:31)
- Ask God, "Will you show me a glimpse behind the scenes of what you are preparing for me?"

Dear Lord Jesus,

Surprise me, Lord! Renew my heart with hope today that you are moving behind the scenes to create a beautiful plan for me. Thank you for all of the ways you have protected and prepared me with your timing. I pray for an acceleration of my promises at just the right time. Help me to embrace your perfect timing in my life in the meantime. Amen.

THE ISSACHAR ANOINTING

> *From the tribe of Issachar, there were 200 leaders of the tribe with their relatives. All these men understood the signs of the times and knew the best course for Israel to take.*
> **1 Chronicles 12:32 NLT**

Imagine having access to a group of anointed leaders who understood God's timing and helped you make the best life decisions. Sounds fantastic, right?

This is exactly the kind of team King David assembled. These men came from the tribe of Issachar and had a unique gift to discern signs and times. Through their wisdom, King David knew the best course for the nation of Israel to take.

The name Issachar is *Yissaskar* (יִשָּׂשכָר) in Hebrew, which means "reward."[1] If we look at the prophetic nature of this name, we can conclude that there is a reward in decoding and following the wisdom of God's timing.

Today, through the power of the Holy Spirit, we can ask God to give us the Issachar anointing—so we have a greater understanding of his timing for our lives.

The Ripe Time

> *For still the vision awaits its appointed time; it hastens to the end—it will not lie. If it seems slow, wait for it; it will surely come; it will not delay.*
> **Habakkuk 2:3 ESV**

A few years ago, I was praying about moving to a new city in Georgia. I was invited to live with new roommates in an up-and-coming part of town. It seemed like the perfect opportunity! The apartments were incredible—nestled near the Chattahoochee River with a coffee shop on the site. It couldn't have been a more dream-like place to call home.

However, as I prayed about moving, I had a dream. I was walking along the Chattahoochee River, and the water was high and dangerous. I approached the river walk and saw fruit trees growing alongside the riverbanks. I looked closer, and I saw the fruit was small and green. It was not yet ripe. I woke up.

I wrote the dream down but wasn't quite sure what it meant. On my way to visit the potential apartment, I had a panic attack on the road. I called my mom for advice.

"This sounds like this opportunity is stressful for you," she said. "Maybe it's not time for you to move."

Reflecting on the dream, I agreed that she was right. While God showed me there was good fruit along the river, it wasn't ripe yet. No one wants to eat unripe fruit!

I decided it wasn't time to move to where the Chattahoochee River flows.

Although I did not move into that apartment, God showed me through my dream that I would live near the Chattahoochee one day when the fruit was ripe.

About a year later, I got invited to join a ministry in another city in Georgia. When I visited to see if it was a good fit, I realized the Chattahoochee River flowed through the town. God called me to live there shortly after my visit, and the purpose of the dream was fulfilled.

Moving to that city changed the trajectory of my life and ministry. God began to open doors for my destiny through my obedience to make the move.

Trusting His Timing

We can easily feel discouraged when we receive a promise from the Lord, but it doesn't come to pass in the time we think that it should.

The truth is a prophetic promise is often given long before its fulfillment. When you catch a glimpse of the promised land, God is giving you a hopeful preview of what's to come so you can prepare ahead of time.

Some promises have a quick turnaround time. If only it could be this way every time! For example, certain kinds of fruit, like strawberries, take only a few weeks to grow. On the other hand, one pineapple needs two whole years to mature and ripen.

While tailor-made God promises may take a little longer to develop, the wait will be worth it once you taste the sweetness of a ripe desire fulfilled.

There is a ripe, right time to receive God's promise for you.

REFLECTION

> *I make known the end from the beginning, from ancient times, what is still to come. I say, 'My purpose will stand, and I will do all that I please.'*
> **Isaiah 46:10**
>
> *As soon as the grain is ripe, he puts the sickle to it, because the harvest has come.*
> **Mark 4:29**

Prophetic Activation: Take time to ask God the following questions and journal his response.

- "Jesus, will you show me any unripe fruit in my life—what is a promise for later timing?"
- "Lord, will you show me what you are currently doing in my life (my ripe fruit)?"

> *Dear Heavenly Father,*
>
> *Thank you for the ripe timing in my life! I ask for increased wisdom and discernment to understand your timing for me. Please reveal to me what is for now in my life, so I won't be idle as I wait. Show me what is for later so I can give your promises time to ripen. Thank you for showing me things to come with the help and power of the Holy Spirit. Bring your right, ripe timing in my life! In Jesus' name, amen.*

THE WAITING ROOM

> *You prepare a feast for me in the presence of my enemies. You honor me by anointing my head with oil. My cup overflows with blessings.*
> **Psalm 23:5 NLT**

Have you ever felt like you are sitting in an endless waiting room?

You prayed and asked God for an appointment—an appointed time for your promise to come to pass.

Yet, you are watching everyone get called ahead of you.

When will he call my name? You wonder.

The clock on the wall keeps ticking, and nothing is changing.

In the wait, despair can start to set in. It's time to get a new perspective. It's time to get free from the heavy weight of disappointment.

While waiting, what if Jesus is turning your dis-appointment into a divine-appointment?

A Latte vs. A Feast

I had a dream I was waiting in line at a coffee shop. The line was moving quickly, but people kept cutting in front of me to get their coffee first. I grew more and more frustrated.

It's just coffee! I thought to myself. *Why is this line taking so long? Why is everyone getting their order before me even though they came after me?*

Finally, my turn came. When I tried to place my simple coffee order, the barista behind the counter said, "We've already been preparing your order for you. It's getting set up over there."

She pointed behind me. I looked and saw a fancy table with chairs, candles, and a bottle of olive oil.

God was revealing to me why my waiting was taking so long. While I was just asking for a simple order, he was setting up an even more elaborate answer to my prayers than I expected. I just wanted a quick coffee—but Jesus was reserving an exquisite feast for me.

Prophetic Encouragement: God's Reserved Promises

I hear the Lord say, "While you wait, I am reserving your promises for you. Although you may feel like you are last in line, watching everyone receive the order they prayed about before you—I want you to know that the last will be first in my perfect timing. I am getting ready to call your name.

> *"So the last will be first, and the first will be last."* **Matthew 20:16**

During your waiting period, you may feel like an olive crushed in the press—but a new anointing is flowing from your life. I will overflow your cup with blessing. I will not give you leftovers, breadcrumbs, or stale bread. I am not giving you fast junk food. I am preparing a bountiful feast beyond your wildest imagination.

Many of my custom-ordered promises take longer to prepare, and yours is in the making. Like winning a coveted spot on a waitlist for a three-star Michelin restaurant, my promise is reserved for you. Your name is on my list of favor!

Don't worry about those who seem to be cutting the line in front of you. I am preparing something more lavish for you. Keep your eyes fixed on me. When I call your name to take your seat and dine with me at the banquet of promise, you will see why the waiting period was so necessary.

In the meantime, your waiting is worship to me. Thank you for trusting me with your heart. I am reserving my very best for you. The waiting is going to be worth it."

REFLECTION

> *Why spend your money on food that does not give you strength? Why pay for food that does you no good? Listen to me, and you will eat what is good. You will enjoy the finest food.*
> **Isaiah 55:2 NLT**
>
> *Wait patiently for the LORD. Be brave and courageous. Yes, wait patiently for the LORD.*
> **Psalm 27:14 NLT**

Prophetic Activation: Take time to read Psalm 23, which talks about God preparing a table in the presence of our enemies. Ask the Lord the following questions and journal his response:

- "Jesus, will you show me a picture of the Psalm 23 banquet table you are preparing for me?"
- "Will you show me what is on your banquet table for me?"

> *Dear Lord Jesus,*
>
> *Thank you for preparing a beautiful feast for me while I wait on you! Help me to stay in line and not settle for anything less than the fullness of what you have for me! Thank you for reserving my promises. Fill my cup to overflowing while I wait. I trust you will call my name at just the right time! Amen.*

MIDNIGHT HOUR MIRACLES

> *"Therefore keep watch because you do not know when the owner of the house will come back—whether in the evening, or at midnight, or when the rooster crows, or at dawn. If he comes suddenly, do not let him find you sleeping. What I say to you, I say to everyone: 'Watch!'"*
> **Mark 13:35-37**

Midnight. The last deadline. The final hour. The end of one day and the beginning of another.

You may feel like you are nearing the midnight hour. You are praying and watching the hands of the clock tick toward midnight, and you wonder if God will come through for you.

When it seems time is running out, Jesus is right on schedule. He usually doesn't move on our timetables, but when he arrives, he is always on time.

The Lord often uses fairytales to speak a message to me, and Cinderella is a special one between me and Jesus. In my own season of waiting, he has used this classic story to strengthen my heart and keep me believing in his promises.

We can glean prophetic insight from the cinder girl's story when we take a closer look.

Cinderella

> *"Even miracles take a little time,"*
> **Fairy Godmother, Cinderella**

In the timeless tale of Cinderella, we meet an unfortunate girl who needs a miracle to go to the ball. She has no dress, no carriage, and no hope of seeing her dream come true.

Out of the blue, her miracle shows up! Her Fairy Godmother comes to her rescue.

Poof! And just like that, her rags transform into a ball gown, her pumpkin becomes a carriage, and she gets a chance to go to the ball.

There's only one problem: she is running incredibly late. She must hurry to make it to the ball in time. However, she is right on time for destiny—she just didn't know it yet.

When Cinderella glides into the ballroom, it seems as if time itself stops. Every eye turns her way—including the one that mattered most. Because she was late, Prince Charming couldn't miss her entrance,

They danced the night away until the clock struck midnight. Although time had officially run out, her miracle was now set in motion. Her chance meeting with the prince led to her becoming a princess. It's the ultimate rags-to-riches story. Cinderella's late arrival changed the course of her fate.

Similarly, our heavenly Father works imperfect situations and delays into perfect timing for us. Like Cinderella, he will lift us from the ashes and seat us with princes (1 Sam. 2:8). He will give us beauty for ashes (Isa. 61:3)—or cinders, if you will.

We must keep believing God can show up at any moment—even if the sand has run out of the hourglass at the midnight hour.

Let's take a look at another miracle that took place at midnight.

Midnight Miracle at the Threshing Floor

In the story of Ruth, we find another woman who is lifted from the ashes into destiny. After losing her husband, Ruth travels with her mother-in-law, Naomi, to Bethlehem.

In need of food, Ruth begins to glean in the barley field of a man named Boaz and wins his favor. When she returns to Naomi, she discovers incredible news: Boaz is their family-redeemer!

After some time passes, Naomi decides it is time for Ruth to find a husband—and she knows the perfect match. To put the plan in motion, she advises Ruth to visit Boaz while he is asleep on the threshing floor.

Through her divine wisdom, Naomi's part in the story can be compared to the role of the Holy Spirit in our lives. She is somewhat like Ruth's own Fairy Godmother.

Ruth follows Naomi's instructions. She sneaks into the threshing floor and lays at Boaz's feet while he is asleep. What a bold move!

> *Around midnight Boaz suddenly woke up and turned over. He was surprised to find a woman lying at his feet! "Who are you?" he asked.*
>
> *"I am your servant Ruth," she replied. "Spread the corner of your covering over me, for you are my family redeemer."*
>
> **Ruth 3:8-10 NLT**

Ruth's midnight move resulted in a miracle. She boldly asks Boaz to fulfill his duty as the family redeemer. He is more than happy to oblige—and marries Ruth!

Ruth goes from gleaning in the field to owning the field.

It's a true Cinderella story—and a miracle set in motion at midnight.

Always Expect a Miracle

You never know how God may be weaving his perfect timing into your life. Imagine the forward ticking of the clock more like the timer counting down to plans of promise—it is bound to go off in God's appointed time.

While you wait, I pray that Jesus would supernaturally increase your faith to hold on. I pray you will come into alignment with his perfect timing for you—not ahead, not behind, but right on schedule.

May you experience a miracle breakthrough when the clock strikes midnight!

REFLECTION

Another Miracle at Midnight

About midnight Paul and Silas were praying and singing hymns to God, and the other prisoners were listening to them. 26Suddenly there was such a violent earthquake that the foundations of the prison were shaken. At once all the prison doors flew open, and everyone's chains came loose. In 2013, I had a dream about God's timing.

Acts 16:25-26

- Have you experienced a time when you received a God breakthrough at the last minute?
- Do you need a midnight-hour miracle in this season?

Dear Holy Spirit,

Thank you for even when it seems you are late, you are right on time! I pray for a heart full of expectation and hope you can show up any minute. Holy Spirit, please give me wisdom and encouragement to be at the right place at the right time. I pray for you to bring my breakthrough even at the midnight hour. In Jesus' name, amen.

MIDNIGHT OIL

> *When the bridegroom was delayed, they all became drowsy and fell asleep. "At midnight they were roused by the shout, 'Look, the bridegroom is coming! Come out and meet him!'*
> **Matthew 25:5-6 NLT**

Imagine the scene. Midnight. A room full of women peacefully sleeping, oil lamps burning low.

Suddenly, a loud voice rings out from the street, "Behold! The bridegroom is coming!"

The women wake with a start and start fumbling in the dark to get dressed. The surprise wedding ceremony is about to start! The bride and her ladies-in-waiting had been waiting many months for this moment, and it was finally here.

However, when they each reach for their oil lamps to see their way in the dark, complete chaos ensues.

"I don't have enough oil for my lamp!" one of the ladies realizes, frantically searching her belongings. Four more ladies are in the same boat.

The other half of the women finish filling their lamps with their own oil as they rush out the door.

"I wish we could help you, but we don't have enough oil for all of us," one of the ladies responds.

Time is running out. Only five women were wise enough to gather enough oil for the groom's surprise arrival.

As the unwise women scramble, the five wise women quickly rush out, the door shutting behind them.

There's no time left—the wedding must begin.

A Prophetic Key in the Traditional Jewish Wedding

The parable of the Ten Virgins in Matthew 25 is a picture of a Jewish wedding custom that would have occurred during Jesus' time.[2]

When a man and woman became engaged, she received the promise that he would marry her after a time of separation and preparation. The catch was—she didn't know the day or hour he would return for her. The wedding would begin immediately upon his arrival!

For about a year, the bridegroom would go to his father's house and prepare a new room for him and his bride to live in once they marry.

When the bridegroom's father inspected the room and deemed it ready, he would tell the son to claim his bride, and the marriage ceremony would commence.

As soon as the father says, "It's time!" the bridegroom doesn't delay. Whether the approval came at mid-morning or midnight, he would go get his bride.

Although the bride may have known a general timeline of the bridegroom's return, she would not know the exact day or hour he would arrive. And this is the scenario taking place with the bridal party in Matthew 25.

The bridegroom's promise stood firm. After a long delay, a midnight miracle takes place. He is finally here to claim his bride! However, his return caught the bridal party by surprise. Only those who prepared with oil during the delay did not miss the wedding day.

This is why we must prepare for our promises, too.

Oil of Intimacy

We can grow tired of waiting for Jesus, our Bridegroom, to show up. We may be tempted to stop believing, praying, and actively watching for him to move in our situations.

During the waiting season, we must fuel the lamps of our hearts with oil. The oil represents our intimacy with Jesus. As we spend time seeking him, he fills us with the oil of intimacy, igniting faith, hope, and love within us. This kind of oil keeps our hearts burning for him even in the darkest, longest night. It gives us light to see when the path to the promise grows dim.

You can't borrow anyone else's oil. No one can cultivate intimacy with Jesus for you or build friendship with him on your behalf. Nor can you give your oil to anyone else. We must seek him ourselves.

So, when it seems like God is delaying the fulfillment of his promises, let your lamp be filled with oil. Stay awake because he can show up any moment. You can go from waiting for it to walking in it overnight.

Take heart; you have a faithful Bridegroom. King Jesus will one day accomplish the ultimate prophetic promise of returning for his Bride—and he will fulfill his personal promises to you.

Supernatural Confirmation

As I finished the final edits on this chapter on April 27, 2024, my friend Shaina texted me out of the blue saying, "'Therefore, stay awake, for you do not know on what day your Lord is coming' (Matt. 24:42). Staying awake with you friend. Midnight oil."

She had no idea I was editing this chapter or that it was called Midnight Oil. Let this be our supernatural sign to believe Jesus is coming to surprise us—it's truly time to get oil and ready for the promises of God.

REFLECTION

The wise ones, however, took oil in jars along with their lamps.
Matthew 25:4

"So you, too, must keep watch! For you do not know the day or hour of my return."
Matthew 25:13 NLT

Recommended Bible reading: Matthew 25

- Would you be ready if Jesus showed up with your promise at the midnight hour? How are you already prepared?
- How can you get ready now and fill your lamp with oil?

Dear Lord Jesus,

Make me ready, Lord! I want to be prepared when you show up at the midnight hour! I need your oil to keep my heart's lamp burning bright. Help me get the oil of intimacy that flows from spending time with you. I pray for a heart full of expectation and hope that you will fulfill every promise to me—even suddenly! Amen.

DARKEST BEFORE THE DAWN

> *God is in the midst of her; she shall not be moved;*
> *God will help her when morning dawns.*
> **Psalm 46:5 ESV**

In 2013, I had a dream about God's timing. Throughout the dream, I couldn't access the gift God had for me until the morning arrived. Angels protected my promises while I waited.

One day in 2020, I pondered the dream. *Jesus, why has the waiting for my promises been so long? Will the morning ever come?*

The next day, I woke up to a text from my friend Danielle.

"God wants you to know the dawn is coming! Dawn means morning, sunrise, break of day, a new beginning!

"Arise, shine, for your light has come,
and the glory of the Lord rises upon you.
See, darkness covers the earth
and thick darkness is over the peoples,
but the Lord rises upon you
and his glory appears over you.
Nations will come to your light,
and kings to the brightness of your dawn.
Isaiah 60:1-3,"* she wrote.

I felt comforted that God heard my questions and was answering them through my friend, but my promises still felt so far away.

Over the next few weeks, I began to hear the phrase 'It's always darkest before the dawn' in the most unusual and random places.

I was in the middle of a conversation with a friend Emily when the song playing quietly in the coffee shop seemed to amplify in my ear, "But it's always darkest before the dawn!"

The Holy Spirit ignited hope in my heart when I heard this phrase. A few days later, I was reading a book when the phrase leaped off the page at me, "In the dark hour before the dawn…"

A few days after that, I was watching a Christmas movie. Suddenly, one of the main characters said, "It's like they say, it's always darkest before the dawn…"

She went on to talk about how we often take matters into our own hands when we can't see that God has angels working behind the scenes of our lives.

I knew God was speaking to me through these repeated divine coincidences and confirmations.

The Dawn is Breaking

I sat on the top of Cadillac Mountain in Acadia National Park in Maine, waiting for the sunrise. As stunning hues of red, pink, and orange began to fill the sky, it's like all creation held its breath at the beauty unfolding.

Watching the breaking of the dawn, I heard the Lord say, "It may be darkest before your dawn right now, but I am at work behind the scenes in your life. I am protecting the promises I have for you. I know the process is hard. I know you can't see how I am going to do it. But a new beginning is on the way. The morning is about to break. Just like this sunrise, your promises fulfilled will be worth the wait. Let this be a sign to you that your dawn is coming!"

How do you hold onto hope when God's promises seem further away than ever? You've waited, prayed, fasted, obeyed, and wondered if you will ever see your answer.

Sometimes, we must press in for a breakthrough until it comes. But there are those special promises that await God's dawn. Our heavenly Father has a moment planned—an appointed time—to set his plans in motion.

Hold fast to the promises of God when it's dark out. Don't give up or lose heart now.

Remember that it is always darkest before the dawn.

The dawn is breaking.

REFLECTION

> *Weeping may stay for the night, but rejoicing comes in the morning.*
> **Psalm 30:5**
>
> *Let the morning bring me word of your unfailing love, for I have put my trust in you. Show me the way I should go, for to you I entrust my life.*
> **Psalm 143:8**

Throughout scripture, ground-breaking, unusual victories often came in the morning. Pick a Bible story to read about a victory at dawn:

- Daniel in the lion's den at dawn: Daniel 6:19-22
- The fall of Jericho at dawn: Joshua 6
- Elisha's servant and God's angel armies at dawn: 2 Kings 6:15-17
- What can you learn about God's nature through this story?

> *Dear Heavenly Father,*
>
> *I declare the dawn is breaking in my situation! Thank you for protecting my promises with your perfect timing in the meantime. I ask for encouragement to hold on when the night feels darkest. Thank you that my weeping will only last for the night—great joy is coming in the morning! In Jesus' name, amen.*

3 KINDS OF SPIRITUAL DELAYS
DIVINE DELAYS

> *"Our friend Lazarus has fallen asleep; but I am going there to wake him up."*
> **John 11:11**

Jesus was late. He arrived in Bethany just in time for his friend Lazarus's funeral. And Martha and Mary were upset about it.

If he had been present, surely Lazarus would have lived!

While it appeared that Jesus missed his divine assignment, there was a miracle in the making.

> *Jesus said, "This sickness will not end in death. No, it is for God's glory so that God's Son may be glorified through it."*
> **John 11:4**

Jesus knew about the outcome of Lazarus' death. Yet, he still purposefully delayed his visit by two more days.

This was a *divine* delay.

If Lazarus hadn't been placed in the tomb, there would have been no need for a miracle.

After all, there must be a death to see God's resurrection power at work.

Yet, even knowing the outcome, Jesus still felt the grief of the moment.

> *Jesus wept.*
> **John 11:35**

Isn't it comforting to know that in the middle of your divine delay, Jesus feels your pain? He has compassion for you.

Finally, with a crowd watching, Jesus rose Lazarus from the grave!

> *Jesus called in a loud voice, "Lazarus, come out!" The dead man came out, his hands and feet wrapped with strips of linen, and a cloth around his face.*
>
> *Jesus said to them, "Take off the grave clothes and let him go."*
> **John 11:43-44**

It was a radical, scandalous miracle! I wonder, when has God intentionally delayed his promises in your life to demonstrate his glory?

A Miracle in the Making

Is there a miracle brewing in the seeming delays in your life?

In the times when you feel abandoned by the Lord, like Martha and Mary felt, you may find Jesus had a plan all along. What if he is preparing a sudden answer to display his glory? His resurrection power can raise any promise from the dark, cold tomb.

With divine delays, God is setting you up for a powerful breakthrough. He knows when to step in at just the right moment.

In the middle of your waiting room, the Miracle-Weaver may have a miracle in the making.

DANIEL DELAYS

> *Then he said, "Don't be afraid, Daniel. Since the first day you began to pray for understanding and to humble yourself before your God, your request has been heard in heaven. I have come in answer to your prayer."*
> **Daniel 10:12 NLT**

In the story of Daniel, we see another kind of delay–a spiritual warfare delay.

As Daniel fasted and prayed, he expectantly waited for God to answer. Meanwhile, he didn't know that a spiritual battle was taking place between the archangel Michael and the principality of Persia. There was a demonic delay blocking his breakthrough.

Through Daniel's faithfulness to seek God, he helped release the spiritual victory in the heavenly realm. The angel finally won the battle and arrived to give God's message to Daniel.

Like Daniel, we may face delays in life due to spiritual warfare. God may lead us to contend in intercession and keep striking the target in prayer and fasting until we see the victory.

Your prayers are a powerful weapon. Do not give up on praying too soon. Your breakthrough could be three weeks, three days, or even three minutes away.

When warfare is delaying your promise from God, you can be confident that you're carrying something genuinely valuable within you. Otherwise, why would a thief attempt to break in to steal, destroy, or delay your promise?

When the enemy is trying to break in and break you down, God will send you a supernatural breakthrough.

What would happen if you didn't give up—and prayed just a little … while … longer?

Divine Interception

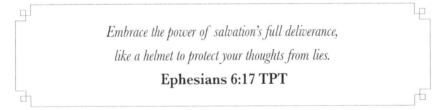

Embrace the power of salvation's full deliverance, like a helmet to protect your thoughts from lies.
Ephesians 6:17 TPT

I went down to the altar during worship and bowed low on my knees.

I felt weary of believing God for his promises.

I was tired of the battle in my thoughts during the delay.

Is this promise truly from God? Have I misheard him? Should I give up praying for a breakthrough?

God often meets me when I bow low in physical expression and come with a humble heart posture before him. I can hear him more clearly in this place of worship, tuning my ear in desperation and hunger to know his heart for me.

I began to see a clear vision taking place. I saw myself as a quarterback running on a football field, wearing a helmet, carrying the football to the goal. I heard the Lord say I needed to wear the helmet of salvation to guard my heart and mind from the enemy's lies.

He said the football game represented my intercession for my promises. My prayers "intercepted" the ball from the enemy. I needed to keep praying until I reached the end goal. A victory was on the way.

While at the altar, a woman laid her hands around my head, making the form of a helmet. She prayed aloud over me, "God, guard her thoughts from the lies of the enemy and renew her mind."

I began to weep even more. She had no idea what the Lord had shown me with the football vision. I felt a heaviness leave as the peace of the Holy Spirit fell on me. God renewed my mind and my spirit that day. He gave me new strength to keep praying and believing during the long delay for my promises.

During Daniel delays, our prayers are powerful to bring a breakthrough. You never know how close you are to the goal. Don't drop the ball. Keep praying until you make the touch down.

> *We demolish arguments and every pretension that sets itself up against the knowledge of God, and we take captive every thought to make it obedient to Christ.* **2 Corinthians 10:4**

JONAH DELAYS

> *"Pick me up and throw me into the sea," he replied, "and it will become calm. I know that it is my fault that this great storm has come upon you."*
>
> **Jonah 1:12**

There are times we may experience a Jonah delay on the way to our God-promises.

Sometimes, we act like Jonah. We delay God's plan due to disobedience.

Other times, someone else in our life is delaying us.

Let's take a look at the story.

Jonah, a Storm, and a Big Fish

As the story goes, God called the prophet Jonah to Nineveh to give a message of repentance—but he didn't want to obey.

He boarded a ship to escape his calling, causing a violent storm. As a result, everyone on the vessel felt the consequences of Jonah's disobedience to God.

The thing is, Jonah knew his actions brought the storm and delayed the boat—yet he still avoided the assignment. As soon as the shipmates threw him overboard, the storm stopped.

Even so, Jonah still wasn't ready to obey—so God brought in Act Two: a giant fish.

In the belly of the whale, Jonah faced the ramifications of his choices again. Yet, this time, his heart reached a place of desperation and humility, and he cried out to God for help.

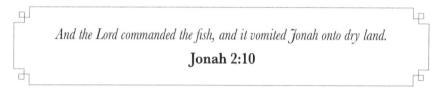

And the Lord commanded the fish, and it vomited Jonah onto dry land.
Jonah 2:10

By the end of his whale adventure, Jonah was ready to obey the Lord and go on his initial assignment to Nineveh.

This is the kindness of God: he pursues us in our disobedience and gives us a second chance. We find unending mercy in his ocean of grace.

God of Second Chances

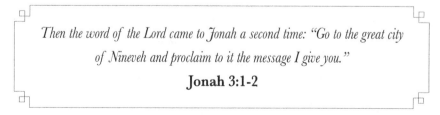

Then the word of the Lord came to Jonah a second time: "Go to the great city of Nineveh and proclaim to it the message I give you."
Jonah 3:1-2

From the story of Jonah, we learn that God is the God of second chances.

While his disobedience delayed God's will from coming to pass, the original assignment for Jonah did not change. God called him a second time, and he obeyed.

He will give us and others in our lives second chances to obey him, too.

Has God asked you to do something, but you haven't obeyed yet? It's never too late to answer the call. You can start today.

Ask Jesus for forgiveness and a second chance to do what he's calling you to do. No matter how challenging the assignment is, God will equip you to complete it.

If there's a Jonah in your life, and you're experiencing the effects of their disobedience, you can pray, "God, teach them to love your will more than their own life so they won't run from it! Encounter them with your love and mercy! Turn their heart of stone into a heart of flesh. Show them the joy of obedience. Let your will be accomplished in their life."

Pray for Jonah's and then release them back to God. He is mighty to save; he is mighty enough to pursue them and transform their hearts in a way only he can. He can get them back on track with his original plan A.

All Delays Work Together for Good

Now the Lord provided a huge fish to swallow Jonah, and Jonah was in the belly of the fish three days and three nights.
Jonah 1:17

Jonah's time in the whale for three days and three nights was a prophetic picture of how our Savior, Jesus Christ, would be in the grave for three days and three nights.

This story reminds us that Jesus paid the price for all of our sins—including our rebellion and disobedience.

As we surrender, repent, and obey the Lord, he will help us step into his plan again. He will redeem the time lost from the delay. He will repair the road back to our promises.

No matter what kind of delay you face—a divine, Daniel, or Jonah delay—God can weave every delay into his beautiful plan for your life.

Keep coming back to him. Pursue his heart. Trust him in the delays.

If you believe, you will see the glory of God.

REFLECTION

When he heard this, Jesus said, "This sickness will not end in death. No, it is for God's glory so that God's Son may be glorified through it."
John 11:4

"Lord, listen! Lord, forgive! Lord, hear and act! For your sake, my God, do not delay, because your city and your people bear your Name."
Daniel 9:19

Jonah obeyed the word of the Lord and went to Nineveh.
Jonah 3:3

Recommended Bible Reading: Luke 11, Daniel 9-10, Jonah 1-4

Prophetic Activation: Are you experiencing a current delay in your promises from God? Which kind? Ask the Holy Spirit to give you a prayer strategy and vision to handle the delays in your life. Write down any plans he gives you.

Dear Heavenly Father,

Break all delay, Lord! Help me to discern how you are working through the delays in my life. I pray for eyes to see when you send a divine delay so I can give you glory. Send supernatural help to break through from every delay that is not from you. Help me obey you so I can step into the flow of your plan for my life. Work all delays together for my good according to Romans 8:28. In Jesus' name, amen.

DIVINE INTERRUPTIONS

Are you ready to obey when Jesus interrupts you?

When we allow God to break into our schedules and lead us in an unexpected way, we might find ourselves in the middle of destiny.

In Luke 5, Jesus interrupted an immovable situation. Simon Peter and the fishermen had been fishing all night with no catch.

> *[Jesus] said to Simon, "Put out into deep water, and let down the nets for a catch." Simon answered, "Master, we've worked hard all night and haven't caught anything. But because you say so, I will let down the nets."*
> **Luke 5:4-5**

As the men obeyed the instruction of Jesus, they caught so many fish that they could hardly bring in their nets! One word from Jesus interrupted their situation. As they obeyed his command, their breakthrough came.

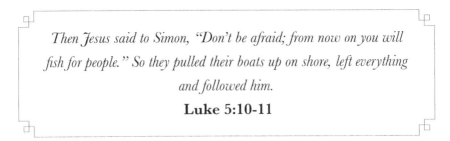

> *Then Jesus said to Simon, "Don't be afraid; from now on you will fish for people." So they pulled their boats up on shore, left everything and followed him.*
> **Luke 5:10-11**

Jesus invited the fishermen to a promise—he would make them fishers of people. When God breaks in, how can we do anything but leave everything to follow him?

The Blue Typewriter

I was sitting in my driveway on the verge of tears. My to-do list sat in the passenger seat next to me. I was performing as the lead in the Shakespeare play *As You Like It*, and I needed to shop for the costumes for our first dress rehearsal. I felt overwhelmed by the daunting task.

Suddenly, the still, small voice of the Holy Spirit interrupted my thoughts, "Go to the coffee shop on 2nd Avenue."

I had a million other things I needed to do that morning that did not involve going to that particular coffee shop. I debated the voice for a few moments in the driveway. *Did I make that voice up? I probably made that up. I don't want to go to the coffee shop. I will see a bunch of people I know and get caught up talking when I have a lot to do today.*

I gave in. I put my car in reverse and started obediently heading down the road.

Walking into the coffee shop, I realized God didn't send me to get a latte. He had a divine appointment waiting for me.

I saw a girl and immediately knew I was supposed to give her a prophetic word. Yes, in the middle of my self-proclaimed difficult day, God gave me grace and genuine joy to encourage someone else. As I introduced myself, I couldn't help but tell her what God wanted her to know.

"I needed to hear that today," she said, tears falling down her face.

We sat sipping coffee and talking for a while. Eventually, I brought up that I was in a Shakespeare play, and I desperately needed to go shopping for my costumes.

"No way!" Lindsey said. "I was actually the artistic designer for Romeo and Juliet here in town recently. I designed all of the costumes for the show!" She pulled out her phone to show me some pictures of their recent production.

"If you want, I would love to go thrift shopping with you and help you pick out your costumes," she said.

I was blown away. In the middle of my stress, God interrupted my plans to bring the exact person I needed who was gifted to solve one of my problems. This is how God works!

We spent the rest of the day at the local Salvation Army, and she helped me pick out costumes for my role as Rosalind. She had a gift for costuming, and something that would have otherwise been challenging became miraculous.

As the day ended, Lindsey said, "There's a gift I feel I am supposed to give you! It's at my apartment across the street."

She ran into her place and came back with a big black case with a handle. When I opened it, I was stunned to find a vintage blue typewriter inside. A few months earlier, I had a vision of a similar blue typewriter. At that time, I heard the Lord say, "I am calling you to write a book."

As I allowed the divine interruption, not only did God take care of my current needs, but he also encouraged me on the pathway to my future prophetic promises. What a kind friend we have in Jesus.

Be Interruptible

As we let Jesus interrupt our plans, his voice often leads us to the very things we seek to find on our own, even down to the most intricate details.

We can stick to our own agendas without tuning into that still, small voice of the Holy Spirit. But imagine the adventures we could go on if we pause, listen, and obey the Holy Spirit—even if he gives an open-ended, random instruction like, "Go to the coffee shop on 2nd Avenue."

Let God divinely interrupt you and change your plans. As you follow him, you may find you are one step closer to your promises.

REFLECTION

> *Many are the plans in the mind of a man, but it is the purpose of the LORD that will stand.*
> **Proverbs 19:21 ESV**

- Have you experienced a divine interruption from God? If so, how did you respond?

- Where else in the Bible did Jesus experience a divine interruption?

- How can you make room in your life for God to interrupt you?

Dear Holy Spirit,

Make me interruptible, Lord! I give you permission to interrupt me when you want to move in my life. Give me a willing heart to obey you! Thank you for increasing my sensitivity to the Holy Spirit's movement in my everyday moments. Fill my heart with holy expectation for what you want to do! In Jesus' name, amen.

FOR SUCH A TIME AS THIS

> *"And who knows but that you have come to your royal position for such a time as this?"*
> **Esther 4:14**

Queen Esther found herself at a pivotal moment. A powerful and wicked man named Haman plotted to destroy her people. The fate of the Jews hung in the balance—and the outcome hinged on her next move.

Yet, God's hidden hand was at work. Esther's cousin, Mordecai, discerned the providential circumstances surrounding the crisis. It was not by mere coincidence that Esther was now the newly appointed queen; it was her divine destiny. She had direct access to the king to save her people.

Her name was fitting for her assignment. Esther means "star" in Persian, and it is thought to have the Hebrew root (סתר) which means "hide" or "conceal."³ She was God's concealed arrow against the enemy, called to arise and shine like a star for such a time as this.

To embolden her in her purpose, Mordecai sent her a message saying, "For if you remain silent at this time, relief and deliverance for the Jews will arise from another place, but you and your father's family will perish. And who knows but that you have come to your royal position for such a time as this?" (Esther 4:13-14).

Answering the call, Esther bravely declared, "If I perish, I perish," (Esther 4:16). She understood her assignment: ask King Xerxes to save her people.

When her hour came to speak up, she faced potential death only to be met with the King's scepter of favor. As a result, God's hidden hand achieved a powerful turnaround through Esther to save the Jewish people. The enemy that sought to kill the Jews met his demise on his own gallows. Against all odds, God brought Esther into her role as queen in his perfect timing.

Your Esther Hour

Like Esther, you are called for such a time as *this*.

Not just someday in the future far away.

Your life has a significant purpose right here, right now. Today.

You may feel hidden and restless, wondering when your name will be called to step into your divine assignment.

The timing of your life is not random. Your current season has a significant purpose. God is preparing you for destiny. His hidden hand has a way of putting us in the right place at the right time—even if it's in a way we would never imagine.

What if living to the fullest now—not someday—sets you up for your future promises? Embracing your current timeline will position you for unprecedented favor for the assignments and calling on your life.

God desires to open your eyes to see what he is doing in your life right now and why he doesn't want you to miss it. There is life to be lived here in the middle of the story.

You are called, chosen, and set apart.

You were born for this hour of history, not another.

Like Esther, God is calling you out of hiding to arise and shine for such a time as this.

My Prayer for You

Dear Heavenly Father,

I pray you would show them the purpose of this current season in their life. Pull back the veil to reveal your beautiful plans you are calling them to step into today, even as you renew life and hope. I pray for your hidden hand to align them with your perfect timing.

In the name of Jesus,

amen.

REFLECTION

He made my mouth like a sharpened sword, in the shadow of his hand he hid me; he made me into a polished arrow and concealed me in his quiver.
Isaiah 49:2

*"Arise, shine, for your light has come,
and the glory of the Lord rises upon you."*
Isaiah 60:1

Recommended Bible Reading: Esther 4

It's time to awaken to your current purpose! Take a moment to ask God the following questions.

- "Dear Heavenly Father, while I await my promises, will you show me where you are already moving in my life?"
- "What is the purpose of my current season?"
- "What three practical goals can I set to achieve my purpose today?"

Dear Heavenly Father,

Thank you for everything you are doing in my life right now! Help me to celebrate what I can see you doing now before the next chapter starts. Please give me wisdom and faith to prepare for what I am praying for. I pray for greater clarity, purpose, and strength to fulfill my purpose today. I declare you have called me for such a time as this! In Jesus' name, amen.

PROPHETIC ENCOURAGEMENT
TRUST HIS TIMING

> *Yes indeed, it won't be long now. God's Decree.*
> *"Things are going to happen so fast your head will swim, one thing fast on the heels of the other. You won't be able to keep up. Everything will be happening at once—and everywhere you look, blessings!"*
> **Amos 9:13 MSG**

I hear the Lord say, "You are not ahead or behind. You are right on time! I have called you for such a time as this. It's time to rise and shine. I am strategically positioning you for my divine kingdom plans.

As you lean into my purpose for you in this season, I will begin to open new doors and pathways you didn't see coming. I have doors with your name on them. I have keys that have been locked away for you to access for such a time as this. Will you come and seek me in the secret place and get the new keys and passcodes for the new doors this season?

In the mystery of my timing, I am shielding you. I want you to rely on my voice and leadership and stay in my timing. I am hiding my plans for you from your enemies—so when you feel anxious, remember there is protection in the mystery of my timing. I have surprise moves. My hidden hand in your life is working all things together for you to arrive at the perfect timing.

Like Esther, will you prepare now for what is still to come? Through the waiting process, I want to anoint you with new anointing oil of promotion and favor that leads to deliverance. I have anointed you with the oil of myrrh, which is the suffering love of my beloved ones who have chosen to follow me through the hard pathways. Though the way of my timing is narrow, I am leading you to the best path of abundant life.

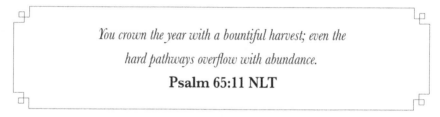

You crown the year with a bountiful harvest; even the hard pathways overflow with abundance.
Psalm 65:11 NLT

My timing is everything. When it's my divine time, you must not hesitate to move into what I am calling you into. Listen for the sound of the alarm and the timer to go off. I have qualified you, so don't worry about the clamor of noise and voices that say you aren't ready for my plans—you don't have time to waste on that! The hour is urgent. This is your Esther hour—your Daniel moment. You will go from preparing to your promotion. Even though you feel behind schedule and hidden, know that you will arrive right on my perfect time, just in time."

PART 5
PROPHESY THE PROMISE

*Fight the Good Fight
on the Battlefield of Faith*

DID GOD REALLY SAY?

> *The serpent was the shrewdest of all the wild animals the LORD God had made. One day he asked the woman, "Did God really say you must not eat the fruit from any of the trees in the garden?"*
> **Genesis 3:1 NLT**

There is a tension in faith between what we believe and what we currently see—the tension of living between what God has said and the fulfillment of it. Will we take him at his word with resolve, or will we bend to entertain that thought, that age-old invitation to deception in a question: "Did God really say?"

The enemy of our souls has no new tricks, but he's still as crafty as ever. From the very beginning in the Garden of Eden, he has been getting us to question God's word to us.

In the waiting, the tension, a better choice still is to be held captive by the voice of the One who spoke the promise.

In a heart posture of awe and surrender, we become most captivated by Jesus—and his voice becomes the strongest echo in our ears.

Every accusation, lie, and doubt begins to fade in the light of his face. And every whisper of the coming promise is evidence of his love for us.

The more we lean into the voice of our Good Shepherd, the more we discern the enemy's taunts as the falsehoods that they are. It's time to lift your heel and crush the head of the serpent trying to keep you from your destiny. The bruises you gain from the fight are your victory marks.

If you don't have a word from God—go get one. Get in your prayer closet, go to a hidden garden, and find a secret place with Jesus.

Ask him for a word, and don't give up until he gives you one. Ask him to repeat it to you, like a song you can't get out of your head. You wake up in the morning, and it's there, already echoing. Rehearse the words until they are engraved in gold on your heart. Don't allow the passage of time or contrary circumstances to make you question the heart of your Father for you.

If Jesus is for you, who can be against you? (Rom. 8:31)

Even if every word were to fall to the ground or unfold in a way you weren't expecting—

He is still infinitely good. Passionately faithful. Endlessly mindful of you.

Will we be among those found faithful, watching for God to answer?

Expect him to come.

Expect him to speak.

Expect him to fulfill his word.

Maybe—just maybe—God really *did* say.

Prophetic Encouragement: Victory is Yours

I hear the Lord say, "Enough is enough! The lying words of the enemy are falling to the ground! Even though the serpent has tried to hinder you with his cunning lies, I will have the final say. It's time to shut the mouth of the false lion, to crush the head of the snake. I am making your enemies my footstool. I am decreeing that your warfare is over!

I will use every attack against you and your promise for your good. Out of the attack will come something sweet for you. I will restore you to more than before. Expect my justice and redemption to come like a wave upon your life as I turn the tides in your favor.

My victory is roaring over you. I am singing songs of deliverance over you in the night. Listen to my voice and take authority over the speaker of lies. In fact, dance in joyful worship, and you'll find the snake trampled beneath your feet as if the battle was an easy walk in the park for you. I am declaring over your life that victory is yours!"

> *"And I will cause hostility between you and the woman, and between your offspring and her offspring. He will strike your head, and you will strike his heel."* Genesis 3:15 NLT

REFLECTION

> *But in that coming day no weapon turned against you will succeed. You will silence every voice raised up to accuse you. These benefits are enjoyed by the servants of the LORD; their vindication will come from me. I, the LORD, have spoken!* **Isaiah 54:17 NLT**

Prophetic Activation: We can identify lies and false beliefs from the enemy by the fruit borne in our lives. Are you bombarded by thoughts and beliefs that make you hopeless, anxious, or afraid? They may be rooted in lies. You can pray the following to uproot any lies and plant truth in your heart.

- "Holy Spirit, will you reveal any lies and false beliefs stealing my hope and joy?"
- "Will you show me the truth you are speaking to me to replace these lies?" Reject these lies aloud and replace them with the truth God speaks to you.

> *Dear Holy Spirit,*
>
> *Your word has the final say! I will listen to your voice above all of the noise. Help me to identify and reject every lie of the enemy trying to steal, kill, and destroy my hope. Thank you that by your Holy Spirit, you empower me to overcome every attempt of the enemy thrown my way. I receive your hopeful words of truth over my life! In Jesus' name, amen.*

PROPHESY THE PROMISE

> *Timothy, my son, I am giving you this command in keeping with the prophecies once made about you, so that by recalling them you may fight the battle well.*
> **1 Timothy 1:18**

A prophetic promise gives us power for battle.

When the pathway to the promised land takes us into the battlefield, a word from God will help us fight the good fight of faith until we see victory.

Six Signs of the Battlefield

You enter the battle when you receive a prophetic promise and then:

1. The opposite of what God said occurs.

2. The waiting is prolonged.
3. No one believes for the promise with you.
4. Everything falls apart.
5. Warfare comes to oppose the word of the Lord.
6. You receive pessimistic reports of giants (obstacles) in the land.

When the promise seems further than ever, the enemy of our souls may come to try to steal, kill, and destroy our hope. We may feel tempted to believe his lies that God will not come through for us. Shut the giant mouth of the crocodile! He speaks nothing but lies.

Remember: God often speaks a word in advance of it coming to pass. The Holy Spirit will show us things that are *still yet* to come (John 16:13). That's why we must not lose hope when we are in the tension between a promise given and its fulfillment. The prophetic word helps us envision the future and make room for it. We walk by faith and not by sight when the word of the Lord is not yet lining up with our current reality.

This is why we take out our prophetic promises and fight the good fight of faith like Paul encouraged Timothy to do. We prophesy his promises.

Five Warfare Strategies

1. **Remember** the promise to strengthen your faith. Recount how God came through for you in past battles.
2. **Pray** to see the word fulfilled.
3. **Prophesy** the promise out loud over yourself and to your situation. You have the authority to prophesy victory in your battles with the word of the Lord.

4. **Declare the opposite**—speak and prophesy life, victory, and breakthrough if your current reality is difficult. For example, if you are facing a storm, declare peace to it. If you are facing a negative report, declare a positive outcome!

5. **Stand firm** in your faith. Put on the whole armor of God and refuse to engage thoughts and words of doubt.

These warfare strategies turn our prophetic promises into stones to defeat our Goliaths. Don't give up—rise up! Fight the good fight of faith until you see the victory!

Spinning with Joy

I have received some of my most significant, on-time prophetic words and promises right before intense spiritual tests and battles in my life. I had no idea when I got the words that something difficult was about to happen—but God knew I would need strength for the battle ahead.

The first prophetic word I ever received came from a girl I barely knew from college. She sent me a message on Facebook saying God gave her a message for me.

"In a vision, I saw you spinning with overflowing joy, your blonde hair twirling in the wind as leaves fell around you. You looked totally free, completely joyful," she said. "The leaves represent things in your life that are about to fall away, but God is saying you can have joy in the middle of the letting go and coming changes."

I was so excited when I read her encouragement! I was new to the prophetic gift and had recently received a powerful baptism in the Holy Spirit.

However, just a few days later, I would go through one of the most significant tests of my life. Her word was about to come to pass in a way I never would have imagined.

It's a long story (a whole separate book in itself), but God brought a revival to my small college—and somehow, my friend Kristina and I received an anointing from the Holy Spirit to help lead it.

What did the revival look like? The Holy Spirit was poured out, and students were powerfully touched by God. The move spread until my whole school heard about it. Over the course of a week, healings, miracles, signs, wonders, salvations, and deliverances broke out. People were lining up for prayer in the school cafeteria. Southern Baptist students began to experience a radical move of the Holy Spirit.

However, the revival came with a costly personal price tag for me. Many of my peers and leaders in the community quickly became offended and confused by the revival—Christians and non-Christians alike. In the midst of the controversy, I chose to stand for the move of God. As a result, I lost most of my friends, my dreams, and my reputation—my life as I knew it.

Like I said, it's a long story.

However, that prophetic word I received right before my battle gave me a light at the end of the tunnel. God knew this was going to happen; he wasn't surprised. He gave me joy in the middle of the battle.

Those things I lost, those leaves that fell to the ground, made room for Jesus Christ to have the first place in my life and bring me into his purpose for me.

Now, I can say I am thankful for the incredible gift God gave me to experience revival. It was worth the price, and I would pay it again. It was a privilege to lose my life to find it in Jesus. Through that experience, God built an unshakeable foundation of faith within me. I have encountered Jesus Christ, and I will never be the same again.

> *What is more, I consider everything a loss because of the surpassing worth of knowing Christ Jesus my Lord, for whose sake I have lost all things. I consider them garbage, that I may gain Christ.*
> **Philippians 3:8**

Fight the Good Fight

Do not be discouraged if you receive a powerful word from God and a battle begins.

The prophetic promise is your weapon.

Wage war with your promise (pray it, declare it, and cling to it) to position yourself for victory. This is your strength training to grow in your authority as a son or daughter of Jesus Christ.

Prophesy the word of the Lord—prophesy your promises until the victory comes.

REFLECTION

> *We demolish arguments and every pretension that sets itself up against the knowledge of God, and we take captive every thought to make it obedient to Christ.* **2 Corinthians 10:5**
>
> *But thanks be to God! He gives us the victory through our Lord Jesus Christ. Therefore, my dear brothers and sisters, stand firm. Let nothing move you.*
> **1 Corinthians 15:57-58**

Prophetic activation: Take a prophetic promise through the five steps: Remember, pray, prophesy, declare the opposite, and stand firm.

> *Dear Heavenly Father,*
>
> *Help me to wage war with my prophetic promises! I choose to remember and believe what you have promised. I pray for it to be accomplished according to your will. I prophesy it is coming to pass! When opposition comes, I will stand firm in the power of your name and embrace the joy of the Lord as my strength. In Jesus' name, amen.*

A GREAT TEST

What do you do when holding fast to a promise—but those closest to you refuse to believe with you?

What if your friends, family, and loved ones offer advice opposite of what God has spoken to you?

Well-meaning people may give us counsel from a pure heart with the right intentions. Their advice might be good, but is it truly from God?

In times like this, the word of the Lord is tested in your life.

Jesus Rebukes Peter

Let's look at a conflict between Jesus and Peter in Matthew 16:21-22: "From that time on Jesus began to explain to his disciples that he must go to Jerusalem and suffer many things at the hands of the elders, the chief priests and the teachers of the law, and that he must be killed and on the third day be raised to life.

Peter took him aside and began to rebuke him. 'Never, Lord!' he said. 'This shall never happen to you!'"

Peter was rightly worried about Jesus. He didn't want him to suffer on the cross. While Peter's opinion seemed logical, he lacked the heavenly revelation to know that Jesus was on his Messianic assignment to lay down his life for the world (John 3:16). In turn, Jesus strongly rebuked Peter:

> *Jesus turned and said to Peter, "Get behind me, Satan! You are a stumbling block to me; you do not have in mind the concerns of God, but merely human concerns."*
> **Matthew 16:23**

Jesus was not going to let anyone persuade him away from his mission. We can learn a lot through how he handled this conflict with Peter.

Jesus and Boundaries

While Jesus set healthy *boundaries*, he didn't put up *walls* with his disciples. Jesus let his followers ask questions and speak their minds openly. Peter felt comfortable sharing his opinions, but Jesus firmly corrected him.

Peter wasn't merely a disciple; he was in the inner circle. Yet, Jesus didn't hesitate to correct his friend. He was not going to be a people-pleaser. He prioritized doing the Father's will above all else. He was unwavering in his identity and assignment.

Despite having a difficult conversation, Jesus did not kick Peter out of his group of followers. He held Peter accountable, forgave, and restored him throughout their relationship.

A GREAT TEST

In today's culture, we often receive advice to cut people out of our lives when conflict arises. However, Jesus teaches us another way—one of maturity, truth, and love.

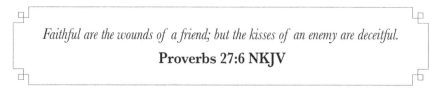

> *Faithful are the wounds of a friend; but the kisses of an enemy are deceitful.*
> **Proverbs 27:6 NKJV**

With that said, there is a caveat: God may occasionally sift people out of our lives who are not meant to come with us on the next level of our journey. When he elevates you, he separates you. We need wisdom to discern the difference between fighting for a relationship and releasing it when God leads us to do so.

Either way, when our promise is tested, we can pass the test by standing on God's word and remaining loving during conflict.

Growing in Wisdom

We need to grow in wisdom to know when to stand firm and set good boundaries around what God has spoken to us. At the same time, we must remember the words of Proverbs 11:14 (NKJV), "Where there is no counsel, the people fall; But in the multitude of counselors there is safety."

Receiving wise counsel from godly, trustworthy people in our communities who support us and pray for us is beneficial. We need to be humble and open to correction and re-direction from those God has placed in our lives to care for us. These kinds of people are a gift. They show us our blind spots, hold us accountable, and speak the truth in love.

Yet, one of the greatest tests comes when these people offer you good advice—but you know it is not God's counsel.

Do not give up when your promise is tested by those closest to you. Stay strong and pray for and forgive those who misunderstand you. You can pass the test.

PRAYER OF FORGIVENESS

> *Be kind to one another, tenderhearted, forgiving one another, as God in Christ forgave you.*
> **Ephesians 4:32 ESV**

Is God asking you to forgive anyone who has hurt you or misunderstood you on your journey? Here is a forgiveness and healing prayer you can put into your own words.

> *Dear Heavenly Father,*
> *I choose to forgive (names) for (offenses), just as you forgive me. I give you all of the pain and hurt they caused me (be specific about what they did and how it impacted you). I ask for you to heal my heart. I ask you to heal my mind and memories, so I no longer dwell on the pain of the past. I let go of all offense, bitterness, and hurt I have held against them. I release them to you now. I invite you, Holy Spirit, to come minister to my heart! I cover myself now with the blood of Jesus, that washes me and sets me free. In the name of Jesus Christ, I pray, amen.*

WAIT FOR THE TRUE PROMISE

> *Now Sarai, Abram's wife, had borne him no children. But she had an Egyptian slave named Hagar; so she said to Abram, "The Lord has kept me from having children. Go, sleep with my slave; perhaps I can build a family through her."*
> **Genesis 16:1-2**

Sarai decided she was tired of waiting for a son. In her advanced age, it now seemed impossible. What if God wouldn't come through on his promises? She encouraged Abram to take matters into his own hands. Instead of waiting on the word of the Lord, he bore a son named Ishmael through their servant Hagar.

While God had mercy on Hagar and blessed Ishmael, he was not the son of promise—he was a counterfeit of the flesh. Even so, the Lord kept his promise despite Abram and Sarai's actions. God blessed them by giving them new identities: Abram became Abraham, a father of many nations, and Sarai became Sarah, a mother of many nations.

Eventually, at the appointed time, Sarah bore Isaac, the true son of promise. They saw the fulfillment of their impossible promise, and their faith was credited to them as righteousness.

However, as Abraham's two sons grew up, the line of Ishmael waged war against the line of Isaac. I wonder what would have happened if Sarai and Abram made a different choice and waited on the true promise of God.

Fool's Gold

While in ministry school, I prayed about moving into a new apartment with new roommates. One night, I dreamed I was walking through the rooms of the new, beautiful living space. I went outside onto the patio and saw gold nuggets scattered on the ground. A sign next to the gold read, "FOOL'S GOLD! TOXIC: DO NOT EAT!"

I did not know how to interpret my dreams at that point in my walk with Jesus, so I didn't understand its meaning. I ended up moving into the apartment and quickly regretted my decision. Unbeknownst to me, it was an extremely toxic living environment. I faced unprecedented spiritual warfare as a result. While the apartment appeared to be a good option, it was a counterfeit of what God truly wanted for me. Only after moving out did I realize he tried to warn me in advance through the dream.

God's warning message in the dream was in the fool's gold. All that glitters is not gold. While the living situation looked "genuine" and ideal on the outside, it was toxic. I was not supposed to choose the fool's gold, but I did.

Although it was a challenging season, the lessons I learned were as valuable as gold to me: pay attention to your dreams and don't fall for the counterfeits of the enemy. Do not take the bait of his fool's gold—wait for the genuine treasure. The wait will be worth it.

The Authentic Vs. a Counterfeit

In our moments of weakness, when we grow weary of waiting, we can be tempted to give up on God. We may go outside his will and choose a counterfeit replacement for his true promise.

According to Merriam-Webster Dictionary, a "counterfeit" is something made in exact imitation of something valuable or important with the intention to deceive or defraud.[1]

The problem with a counterfeit is that it often resembles the authentic thing. The definition emphasizes an "exact imitation" of something valuable, making it difficult to discern the difference. However, another crucial aspect is highlighted in the definition: a counterfeit is designed to deceive.

Counterfeits are one of the tactics deployed by the enemy of our souls, the father of lies. He often presents us with a counterfeit right before the real deal to throw us off God's track. Although a counterfeit closely imitates the genuine, we may sense a subtle unease in our spirit, signaling something is wrong. This is why we must pray for discernment to distinguish between what is counterfeit and genuine and what is good from evil.

> *But solid food is for the mature, who by constant use have trained themselves to distinguish good from evil.*
> **Hebrews 5:14**

We have access to a much-needed gift of the Holy Spirit mentioned in 1 Corinthians 12:10 to help us: the gift of discerning of spirits. The Greek word used to describe this gift of discernment is *diakrisis*, defined as a thorough judgment (a discernment or conclusion) that distinguishes "look-alikes."[2]

As you ask him, God will give you the ability to distinguish between his authentic promise and the false "look-alikes," safeguarding you from deception. Pray for the gift of discernment and pay attention to the promptings of the Holy Spirit, giving you wisdom and insight for life.

Our Redeemer Lives

On this path to God's promises, we sometimes make mistakes and regret our decisions. We choose to take matters into our own hands out of our own free will. We choose a counterfeit over the true promise God has for us.

If you have found yourself in this position, know that Jesus Christ is your Redeemer. He can redeem any plan or promise when we go astray. Like he did for Abraham and Sarah, he can still fulfill his promises for you!

My charge to you is this: wait on the Lord. Listen for his voice. Continue to seek his will in all things. Pray for discernment. When the enemy of our souls comes to deceive us with an "exact imitation" of the promise, resist him and stand firm.

Remember in your moments of weakness that God is faithful to keep his promises to you. Do not create a counterfeit Ishmael. Do not eat the fool's gold. Do not settle for less than God's best. Your authentic promises from God are coming.

REFLECTION

> *For it is written that Abraham had two sons, one by the slave woman and the other by the free woman. His son by the slave woman was born according to the flesh, but his son by the free woman was born through the promise.*
> **Galatians 4:22-23**

- Have you ever felt tempted to choose a counterfeit over waiting for God's promises?
- Can you recall a time when God gave you warnings and discernment regarding a situation that required his insight?

Dear Heavenly Father,

Protect me from all counterfeits! I pray for the gift of discernment to distinguish between the genuine and the false, good and evil in my life. Please redeem any "look-alikes" I have chosen or created out of my own free will. Help me to walk in the Holy Spirit and not in my flesh, so I can inherit the promises you have for me! Thank you for being faithful to fulfill your promises to me! In Jesus' name, amen.

DON'T TEASE ME

> *"Did I ask for a son, master? Didn't I tell you,*
> *'Don't tease me with false hopes'?"*
> **2 Kings 4:28 MSG**

Let these truths sink into your heart:

God's promises are not wishful thinking.

His words are not a book of false hopes.

He is not teasing you with his promises.

God is not like people who easily change their minds and don't follow through on their word.

However, in the long waiting seasons, it can feel like he is doing just that—teasing us with his promises.

In 2 Kings 4, we meet the Shunamite woman. She hosts Elisha in her home, and he asks how he can help her in response to her kindness.

> *"What can be done for her?" Elisha asked.*
>
> *Gehazi said, "She has no son, and her husband is old."*
>
> *Then Elisha said, "Call her." So he called her, and she stood in the doorway.*
>
> *"About this time next year," Elisha said, "you will hold a son in your arms."*
>
> *"No, my lord!" she objected. "Please, man of God, don't mislead your servant!"*
>
> *But the woman became pregnant, and the next year about that same time she gave birth to a son, just as Elisha had told her.*
>
> **2 Kings 4:14-17**

God fulfilled the impossible word he spoke to the Shunamite woman.

Brave Enough to Hope

How often do we feel like the Shunamite woman in the process of God's promises? *Don't tease me, Lord! Don't mislead me with false hopes!*

When the waiting is long and hard, hearing God promise us the impossible can confront our cynicism and loss of hope. When we get our hopes up, we may fear they will come crashing down.

That's why it is brave to hope. And that's exactly what God is calling us to do. After all, hope is the breeding ground of miracles. Jesus can use even the smallest seed of hope to plant and grow a harvest of answered prayer.

So, remember: God doesn't promise without an intention to fulfill. A prophetic promise is not a carrot on a string or a trail of breadcrumbs leading down a dead-end path. His words aren't wishful thinking or false hopes. Every promise is yes and amen in Jesus Christ.

REFLECTION

> *How precious to me are your thoughts, God!*
> *How vast is the sum of them!*
> *Were I to count them, they would outnumber the grains of sand—*
> *When I awake, I am still with you.*
> **Psalm 139:17-18**

Prophetic Activation: Have you felt teased with God's promises? I encourage you to read Psalm 139. Take a moment to exchange those thoughts for God's truths by using the listening prayer below.

Dear Lord Jesus,

I have felt teased with your promises. I surrender this thought to you at the foot of the Cross. Will you tell me the truth about your promises for me? What is a precious, true thought you are thinking about me according to Psalm 139? (Listen for the Holy Spirit's response and write down the truths he speaks.) I give you any bitterness and disappointment from my journey. What do you want to give me in exchange for these things? (Listen for the Holy Spirit's response and write down the truths he speaks.) Please heal my heart in the deepest places of pain. Thank you for the breakthrough that is coming! Amen.

FORGET-ME-NOT

> *In her deep anguish Hannah prayed to the Lord, weeping bitterly. And she made a vow, saying, "Lord Almighty, if you will only look on your servant's misery and remember me, and not forget your servant but give her a son, then I will give him to the Lord for all the days of his life..."*
> **1 Samuel 1:10-11**

If anyone knew about the anguish of waiting for a promise, it was Hannah.

Hannah wanted a child more than anything. She sought the Lord year after year, but her situation stayed the same. To make matters worse, her rival, Peninnah, would constantly taunt her because she had a child—but Hannah did not.

Yet, even though Hannah lived in hope deferred, she still found the strength to continue to go to the temple and worship God. What a beautiful sacrifice we offer him when we praise through suffering.

Finally, Hannah broke down. She wept uncontrollably and prayed in such a bitter way that Eli thought she was drunk.

She cried out, "Lord, forget me not!" Little did Hannah know her breaking point was her tipping point. Her answer to prayer was set in motion.

I want to point out a few details from her story. First, there wasn't a specific moment before this where we see God directly promising her a child—it was simply the desire of her heart.

Secondly, God didn't rebuke Hannah for praying for a child. He didn't tell her to focus only on him and forget her heart's desires. He didn't tell her that her desire was idolatry. Hannah desired a *good* thing from the Lord.

Finally, her desperate cries broke through to heaven, and God honored her request.

And the Lord remembered her. 1 Samuel 1:19

Miraculously, Hannah became pregnant and gave birth to a son. In 1 Samuel 1:20 it says, she named him Samuel, saying, "Because I asked the Lord for him."

The Hebrew name *Samuel* means "heard by God."[3] Not only was Hannah heard by God, but her son Samuel became one who heard God.

She didn't just receive a son—she birthed a prophet who would impact the nation of Israel. The answer to her prayers gained interest in her waiting. Samuel needed to be born at the right point in history to fulfill his destiny. When God seemed late, perhaps his delivery was right on time. The Lord remembered Hannah, and her story has been remembered for generations.

The God Who Remembers

Many times throughout biblical history, men and women of faith had a divine moment when the Lord "remembered" them.

Like Noah. (Gen. 8:1)

Like Sarah. (Gen. 21:1)

Like Hannah. (1 Sam. 1:19)

To be remembered, one must at least seem forgotten for a time.

Maybe it is not so much that the Lord *forgets*...

He is *always* remembering you. When God remembers, perhaps it speaks of the appointed time to answer our prayers.

Prophetic Encouragement: He Will Forget-You-Not

While praying, I saw a picture of Jesus gathering forget-me-not flowers and creating crowns for those who have felt forgotten this season.

I saw many crying out like Hannah, desperate for God to shift their situation. Many hear the taunts of their rival, the enemy of their souls, to discourage them and keep them from believing the Lord for a breakthrough. God is destroying accusation and comparison to set you free. God remembered Hannah, and he will remember you!

When your answer to prayer seems delayed, prepare for a more significant God testimony than you can imagine. Your prayers are gathering in the heavens like a heavy storm cloud, waiting for the dew point to reach the due time. Your due date is on the calendar!

Many powerful women in the Bible faced barrenness. However, these women didn't give up, even during their breaking points. Not only did God perform a miracle and answer these women by giving them children, but he also gave them children with extraordinary callings and stories that still impact us today.

God took barren situations and made history. He didn't just answer—he created a legacy of miracles.

Here is a list of women in the Bible who saw a miracle from God:

- Sarah gave birth to Isaac.
- Hannah gave birth to Samuel.
- Rebekah gave birth to Jacob and Esau.
- Rachel gave birth to Joseph.
- Manoah's wife gave birth to Samson.
- The Shunamite woman gave birth to a son.
- Elizabeth gave birth to John.

May their stories renew your hope today that nothing is too hard for God.

There is a downpour of blessings coming. Jesus is catching your tears in a bottle. As your tears burst forth, heaven is paying attention.

In the groanings and anguish of your prayers—your intercession in the heavenly throne room—a tipping point is coming. When you reach your breaking point, you will break through.

God will forget-you-not.

REFLECTION

> *But Zion said, "The Lord has forsaken me,*
> *the Lord has forgotten me."*
> *Can a mother forget the baby at her breast and have no compassion on the child she has borne?*
> *Though she may forget, I will not forget you!*
> *See, I have engraved you on the palms of my hands ;your walls are ever before me.*
> **Isaiah 49:14-16**

- Do you remember the last time God answered one of your prayer requests? Take a moment to thank him for what he has already done. Make petitions and requests for what you are believing the Lord for now.

Dear Lord Jesus,

I am crying out to you like Hannah! Will you come quickly with an answer to my requests? I am desperate for you to move, Lord! Thank you for listening to me every time I call. Thank you that you don't despise the desires of my heart, but you long to be gracious to me! I thank you that at the right time, you will remember me. I will keep worshiping you while I wait! Amen.

WHERE YOU GO, I WILL GO
RUTH'S STORY

The book of Ruth begins with a tragic ending. Naomi's husband and two sons have died, leaving her daughters-in-law, Ruth and Orpah, without husbands.

Thus, Ruth found herself at a crossroads.

She faced a pivotal decision: would she stay in her homeland of Moab and start over? Or would she follow Naomi, her mother-in-law, into an unknown land?

Ruth decides to be brave. She tells Naomi, "Where you go I will go, and where you stay I will stay. Your people will be my people and your God my God" (Ruth 1:16).

There was no turning back for Ruth. She made up her mind. She chose to forsake all she knew and followed the one true living God.

Little did she know her faithfulness would position her for a beautiful promise.

Right Place, Right Time

In the very next chapter, God's hidden hand begins to turn tragedy into triumph.

It just so happens that Naomi and Ruth arrive in Bethlehem at the start of the barley harvest.

It just so happens that Ruth stumbles into the barley field of a man named Boaz.

> *So Ruth went out to gather grain behind the harvesters. And as it happened, she found herself working in a field that belonged to Boaz, the relative of her father-in-law, Elimelech.*
> **Ruth 2:3 NLT**

The word for "happened" in this passage is the Hebrew word *qarah*, which speaks of a providential circumstance—an encounter from being in the right place at the right time.[4]

There is no Hebrew word for coincidence. God's hidden hand orchestrated the timing of the women's arrival in Bethlehem. His providence placed Ruth in Boaz's field.

It just so happened that a story of loss turned into a beautiful, redemptive love story.

Ultimately, this divine *qarah* moment leads to Boaz becoming Ruth's kinsman-redeemer. As a result, Naomi and Ruth now had provision and protection for life. What's more, Ruth and Boaz have a son named Obed, who becomes the grandfather of King David. From the line of King David came the Messiah, Jesus Christ.

Don't Turn Back to Moab

When the road to God's promises becomes rocky and uncertain, we have a choice to make, like Ruth.

Will we continue to follow Jesus, no matter the cost?

Or will we turn back to Moab?

Moab was an idolatrous nation that didn't follow the Lord. Naomi and her family ended up in Moab in the first place because of a famine in Bethlehem. They didn't trust the Lord to provide, so they left home for a country that could supply food. Moab represents rebellion, disobedience, and following other gods.

Turning back to the familiar may seem tempting, but we must resolve not to return to what God delivered us from.

When we face an unexpected crossroads, let us be brave like Ruth and vow to Jesus, "Where you go, I will go, and where you stay, I will stay."

As we do, we may find ourselves perfectly positioned for his promises.

God will weave *qarah* moments into our lives, putting us directly in the field of our dreams. We will find ourselves safe under the shadow of His wings.

When it seems like the end, keep going, keep following Jesus. The end of a familiar road is your new beginning.

Your promises from God await you, just ahead.

REFLECTION

> "May the LORD repay you for what you have done. May you be richly rewarded by the LORD, the God of Israel, under whose wings you have come to take refuge."
> **Ruth 2:12**
>
> Whoever finds their life will lose it, and whoever loses their life for my sake will find it.
> **Matthew 10:39**

- Like Ruth, have you had to make a tough decision to follow Jesus when you could have chosen another route?
- When has God placed you in the right place at the right time?

Dear Lord Jesus,

I want to follow you my whole life! Thank you for making a way when I reach a dead end. Thank you for leading me to your best path when I reach a crossroads. Please position me at the right place at the right time for my promises. Thank you for turning around my situation quickly! Fill me with new hope as I keep moving forward. Amen.

BITTERSWEET
NAOMI'S STORY

> *"Don't call me Naomi,"* she told them. *"Call me Mara, because the Almighty has made my life very bitter."*
> **Ruth 1:20**

With nothing left in Moab, Naomi travels with Ruth back to Bethlehem, where they face an unknown future together.

In her pain, Naomi says, "Just call me Marah," which means "bitter." She couldn't see that God was setting the stage for a beautiful new beginning.

Divine Turn Around

When the women arrive in Bethlehem, everything turns around

for the better. Through divine providence, Boaz becomes their family redeemer, becoming a husband for Ruth and providing for her and Naomi for the rest of their lives.

God restored seven times to Naomi what she lost.

> *The women said to Naomi: "Praise be to the Lord, who this day has not left you without a guardian-redeemer. May he become famous throughout Israel! He will renew your life and sustain you in your old age. For your daughter-in-law, who loves you and who is better to you than seven sons, has given him birth."*
> **Ruth 4:14-15**

God turned a bitter tragedy into a lasting legacy—and it didn't take long at all.

The Lord Our Healer

From Naomi, we learn it's not the end of our story when we face loss, difficulty, and disappointment.

We can often feel like Naomi when we go through hard times—our bitter circumstances become our identity. We put on hopelessness like a heavy coat and wear it everywhere we go.

In our pain, we may say, "Just call me Bitter."

However, the Lord wants to turn all of the bitterness in our lives into sweetness.

Before Naomi's story, the name Marah appears in another place in the Bible. In Exodus 15, the children of Israel are thirsty as they wander in the desert, and they think they have arrived at an oasis.

> *When they came to the oasis of Marah, the water was too bitter to drink. So they called the place Marah (which means "bitter"). Then the people complained and turned against Moses.*
>
> *"What are we going to drink?" they demanded. So Moses cried out to the Lord for help, and the Lord showed him a piece of wood. Moses threw it into the water, and this made the water good to drink.*
> **Exodus 15:23-25**

In this miracle moment, God revealed himself as Jehovah Rapha, the God Who Heals, because he healed the bitter water and made it sweet so the people could drink.

God healed the bitter waters of Marah.

He healed Naomi's bitterness into sweetness.

Jesus Christ will heal all of our bitterness, too.

Like Moses threw the piece of wood, Jesus will take the wooden cross of Calvary and stir the bitter waters of our lives, turning them sweet.

He will carefully weave his hidden hand into our stories to turn it all around just in time.

May your next chapter begin with, *"And it just so happened …"*

With God, if it's not sweet, it's not the end.

We just have to keep going.

REFLECTION

> *And hope does not put us to shame, because God's love has been poured out into our hearts through the Holy Spirit, who has been given to us.*
> **Romans 5:5**

Recommended Bible Reading: Book of Ruth, Exodus 15:22-26

Prophetic Activation: Have you felt like Naomi and let your temporary circumstances define you?

- Ask the Holy Spirit to help you identify any false labels you have taken on as your identity. Do you feel bitter, unworthy, alone, or unlovable?
- Surrender those labels to Jesus and ask him to tell you what true labels he gives your identity (Examples: worthy, protected, and loved).

Dear Heavenly Father,

Thank you for turning all of my bitterness sweet! I want to know you as Jehovah Rapha, the God Who Heals me! Help me to have faith and hope that it's not the end of the story when I go through loss and disappointment. Help me be at the right place and time to experience your hidden hand at work in my life! In Jesus' name, amen.

GOD WILL BLESS THE BROKEN ROAD

> *The LORD blessed the latter part of Job's life more than the former part.*
> **Job 42:12**

On this road to the promised land, we may encounter great loss and heartache. We may feel like Job, enduring test after test until we have nothing left. The promise may seem beyond repair.

We may be left wondering, "Why me, God? Where are you in the middle of my suffering? Did you forget about me? Is there any hope for my future after all of the suffering I have gone through?"

When it feels like the storms of life have wiped every promise away, our hope can remain anchored in the unshakeable love of our heavenly Father.

He is not finished with your story.

Have you heard the song *God Bless the Broken Road* by Rascal Flatts?

This song is a beautiful metaphor for God using the losses, heartbreaks, and twists we face to lead us into his beautiful blessings for our lives.

Perhaps God is using your broken road to lead you straight into his perfect will. What if your biggest blessings are right around the corner?

While the enemy of your soul would want you to believe the false narrative that God has let you down and forsaken you, Jesus is authoring another story about your journey.

Prophetic Encouragement: Your Story Isn't Over

> *And we know that in all things God works for the good of those who love him, who have been called according to his purpose.* **Romans 8:28**

Hear the Lord say to you today, "I am working all things together for your good. I will let nothing go wasted in your life. I will do exceedingly and abundantly beyond all you can ask, think, or imagine (Eph 3:20). I have led you step by step this far, and I will not abandon you now.

> *"And surely I am with you always, to the very end of the age."*
> **Matthew 28:20**

I know you may want to give up on this journey. You will wonder if you heard my voice calling you in the first place. You will wonder if there is an easier path or if you should just go your own way. You may face disappointment, heartache, and fear. Yet, while your promise gets tested in the fiery trials of life, one promise has stood the test of time—I have promised to be with you. You are never alone.

> *The LORD himself goes before you and will be with you; he will never leave you nor forsake you. Do not be afraid; do not be discouraged.*
> **Deuteronomy 31:8**

When the burden gets too heavy for you, exchange your heavy yoke for my light burden. When the battle intensifies, I am your shield and your reward. I am covering you under the shadow of my wings. When others misunderstand you, I perfectly understand your heart. I am embracing you right here in this moment.

I am pouring a fresh oil of joy over you to give you new strength. I am picking you up from the ashes and placing a new crown of victory on your head. I am binding up every broken place in your heart. Receive my supernatural hope to keep going.

I am the Author and Finisher of your faith—your story isn't over. I have a new chapter coming for you. Stay close to me, and I will carry you across the finish line. In the meantime, come to me, and I will provide you with everything you need.

I know you've been expecting the outcome of your promise to look a certain way. But will you trust me as the old falls away so the new can come? My best is on the way. I will turn the bitter into sweet!

On your broken road, you'll be astonished as I open new doors that couldn't be cracked open any sooner. I will take your dis-appointments and turn them into my divine appointments! I am bringing you into perfect alignment so you can possess the promise I have for you.

I know you better than you know yourself—I know exactly what you need today. I love you more than you can fathom. Like the cardinals I watch over every morning, noon, and night, I will take care of and provide for you.

While the pathway to my promises will hold mysterious twists and turns, joys, and at times, disappointments, my truth over your life will prevail.

> *"For I know the plans I have for you,"* declares the Lord, *"Plans to prosper you and not to harm you, plans to give you hope and a future."*
> **Jeremiah 29:11**

My best for you is yet to come. Lean into my love for you today."

My Prayer for You

If you have been in a season of suffering loss, I pray that God renews your hope and faith today. You will see the Lord's goodness in the land of the living. I pray he will redeem the years the locusts have stolen and restore you to better than before.

I pray that the latter part of your journey will be even more blessed than the former part! I pray that you will have new eyes of hope to see that with Jesus by your side, the best is yet to come. Amen.

REFLECTION

He will wipe every tear from their eyes. There will be no more death or mourning or crying or pain, for the old order of things has passed away.
Revelation 21:4

I consider that our present sufferings are not worth comparing with the glory that will be revealed in us.
Romans 8:18

I remain confident of this: I will see the goodness of the LORD in the land of the living.
Psalm 27:13

Recommended Bible Reading: Job 42:10-17, Romans 8:18-30

Prophetic Activation: Do you need healing from a time of loss and tragedy? Invite Jesus into your process and pour out your heart to him. Ask him to release a blessing in place of what you have lost.

- "Jesus, what blessings do you have in store for my future?"
- Write down his blessing and pray it over yourself.

Dear Lord Jesus,

I need you! As I draw close to you, draw close to me in the middle of my losses and heartaches. Please renew my hope for the future. I invite you to come in and heal my heart in the deepest places of wounding. Thank you that my mourning will turn to joy in the morning. Make me ready to receive the beautiful blessings you are preparing for me! Amen.

PART 6
GOLD REFINED BY FIRE

The Testing of our Hearts and the Promise

*The crucible for silver and the furnace for gold,
but the Lord tests the heart.*
Proverbs 17:3

REFINER'S IMAGE

> *He will sit as a refiner and purifier of silver; he will purify the Levites and refine them like gold and silver.*
> **Malachi 3:3**

Imagine the Father as a skilled silversmith.

He carefully, gingerly takes the raw silver and dips it in the refiner's fire.

Radiant flames dance in his eyes as he keeps his gaze fixed on the work before him.

One moment too long in the heat, and the silver will be ruined.

Within the hottest heart of the flames, black soot begins to melt away.

Finally, the silver has been refined so purely that he can see his image reflected in the precious metal.

Now, he knows it's time to remove the purified silver from the refiner's pot.

He proudly examines the beautiful masterpiece he has created.

It shimmers beautifully in the light of the fire, and he couldn't be more pleased.

His work is complete.

And this is the process our Father God takes us through, too.

When he calls you and gives you a promise, make no mistake—

He may lead you into the refiner's fire.

This is not to hurt you or confuse you. It's to prepare you to be one who can hold the promise he has for you.

In the heat of the flames, he purifies your character so deeply that you can be entrusted with the heavy glory and anointing of his calling on your life.

He is transforming you more and more into the image of Jesus.

When you have been tested in the wilderness and purified in the refiner's fire—your faith will prove as genuine as gold.

REFLECTION

> *In all this you greatly rejoice, though now for a little while you may have had to suffer grief in all kinds of trials. These have come so that the proven genuineness of your faith—of greater worth than gold, which perishes even though refined by fire—may result in praise, glory and honor when Jesus Christ is revealed.*
> **1 Peter 1:6-7**

- Can you remember a time you endured the refiner's fire?
- What lessons did you learn about yourself and God through the refining process?

> *Dear Heavenly Father,*
>
> *Give me the grace to endure the refining process. Help me to lean into what you are doing in my life and not retreat. Thank you for using your refiner's fire to purify my heart and make me more like Jesus. I pray my faith will prove as genuine as gold on the other side of the fire. In Jesus' name, amen.*

FROM THE PIT TO THE PALACE

> *Until the time came to fulfill his dreams, the LORD tested Joseph's character.*
> **Psalm 105:19 NLT**

If anyone knows about the refining fire of a prophetic promise, it's Joseph. At the start of his story, we learn he is Jacob's favorite son. His father even made him an ornate robe of many colors to signify his favor, stirring jealousy in his eleven brothers.

However, Joseph wasn't solely favored by Jacob—he was favored by God. This became evident when Joseph received two prophetic dreams, revealing a promise: he would one day rule in a position of power over his family.

However, the dreams made Joseph's eleven brothers hate him even more.

FROM THE PIT TO THE PALACE

They plotted to sabotage his dreams.

They stripped away his rainbow robes, representing God's promises.

They threw him in a pit and sold him into slavery.

Then, Joseph landed in prison for a crime he didn't commit.

When it looked like his dreams were dashed, the word of the Lord tested Joseph. Alone in his prison cell, he likely wondered, *Did I truly hear God about my future? Will my dreams ever come to pass?*

Yet, there must have been an ember of hope glowing in his heart. He still interpreted the dreams of the Butler and the Baker when he could have entirely written off the power of dreams altogether. He had been waiting a decade and his dreams had yet to come to pass. Why would he bother helping others understand their own? Nonetheless, Joseph still cultivated the gift of dream interpretation. He still believed that his dreams would come true. God's promises to Joseph still awaited the appointed time.

After years of testing, Joseph's divine moment arrived. Pharaoh heard about his ability to interpret dreams and summoned him from prison. Joseph's faithfulness to steward his gift paid off, and he accurately interpreted Pharaoh's dreams. He discerned that seven years of famine were coming to the region, but they had seven years of plenty to prepare. As a result, Pharaoh promoted Joseph to second in command over Egypt, launching him from the prison to the palace overnight.

As famine hit the land, Joseph's brothers traveled to Egypt in search of food. When they arrived, they didn't recognize Joseph–but he recognized them. They bowed down to him, fulfilling the prophetic dreams he had of them years earlier.

In a powerful plot twist, Joseph revealed his true identity and chose to forgive his brothers, a testament to God's refining of his character. He was able to see God's bigger plan through the path of testing to the promise. He said to his brothers, "As for you, you meant evil against me, but God meant it for good, to bring it about that many people should be kept alive, as they are today" (Gen. 50:20).

Against all hope, Joseph's dreams finally came to pass. God restored his family and everything he lost, erasing the pain of his past and blessing his future.

God Meant it for Good

From Joseph's journey, we can find comfort in this truth: when God makes a promise, he will be the one to fulfill it at the appointed time. No obstacle can stop it. No person can block it. We can't even sabotage a true God promise if we stay in the refining fire.

Think about this: what if God has factored in every twist, turn, and detour of your journey in advance to get you to his promises right on time? If you find yourself in a pit or prison, be encouraged that you may be on the very launching pad of your destiny.

As Joseph realized at the end of his testing, God will turn everything meant for evil against you for your ultimate good. He will pour on us a healing balm of Gilead—a supernatural anointing for heart healing—to help us through the painful process to the promise.

If you are going through significant testing in life, it must mean there is a beautiful treasure at the finish line. Even as God prepares your promise, he is refining you like a diamond. He's making you look more like Jesus in the process—and how beautiful you are becoming.

REFLECTION

> *And we know that in all things God works for the good of those who love him, who have been called according to his purpose.*
> **Romans 8:28**

- Can you relate to any part of Joseph's story?
- How is God refining your character in this season?
- How can you be faithful to serve Jesus in this season while you await promises?

Dear Lord Jesus,

I pray that nothing will stop the purposes, dreams, and promises you have for my life. Finish your work in my heart and character so I am ready for the fulfillment of my promises at the right time! Thank you for taking everything meant against me for harm and working it all for my ultimate good. Amen.

THE LORD WILL PROVIDE

> *So Abraham called that place The Lord Will Provide. And to this day it is said, "On the mountain of the Lord it will be provided."*
> **Genesis 22:14**

Imagine Abraham reaching the top of Mount Moriah with his son, Isaac.

Isaac, meaning laughter. Every time his name was spoken, it served as a reminder that Sarah laughed when God promised her a son in her old age. Against all odds, God fulfilled his word.

Yet, after decades of waiting, the Lord was now asking Abraham to sacrifice his only son. Was he willing to let go of his long-awaited promise?

Abraham obeyed and began to prepare the altar to offer Isaac.

But something unexpected happened ... The angel of the Lord interrupted him and told him not to do it! It was a test of Abraham's heart—and he passed!

At that moment, God provided another sacrifice, a ram, to preserve the promise. So, Abraham called the place the Lord will Provide.

When we obey, God always gives us exactly what we need when we need it.

Pass the Test

Like Abraham, God will test our hearts, too. There may come a moment when he asks us to lay down our promise on the altar.

Yes, after all the waiting, believing, and praying ...

Jesus asks us to let go.

In the fires of testing, we can cling to an anchored truth: when we obediently surrender our promise to Jesus, he will always provide what we need in return.

Letting go of the promise isn't the only way God may test us. He may ask us to do any number of challenging things:

Forgive and show love to someone who has hurt us.

Give generously to others when it feels we have run dry.

Take the leap of faith before we know where we will land.

When testing comes, remember God's track record of faithfulness throughout biblical history and your own history in him.

He was faithful to Abraham. He was faithful to Sarah. He will be faithful to you.

He has good intentions for you through the testing you go through. When he requires your obedience, he will empower you to pass the test.

May your testimony be, "It was worth it to obey the Lord! He provided me exactly what I needed at the right moment."

REFLECTION

> *The LORD's promises are pure, like silver refined in a furnace, purified seven times over.*
> **Psalm 12:6 NLT**

> *Against all hope, Abraham in hope believed and so became the father of many nations, just as it had been said to him, "So shall your offspring be."*
> **Romans 4:18**

Recommended Bible Reading: Genesis 22:9-19

- When has God asked you to obey him in a costly or challenging way?
- Has God asked you to lay your promise on the altar? How did you respond?

Dear Heavenly Father,

Help me trust you more deeply and pass every test that comes my way. Like it says in Psalm 51:12, restore to me the joy of your salvation, and make me willing to obey you. Help me to trust you will give me exactly what I need when I need it when I am willing to surrender and obey you. Thank you that my promises are always safest in your hands. In Jesus' name, amen.

A HEAVY CARRIAGE LOAD

> *Listen to me, you descendants of Jacob, all the remnant of the people of Israel, you whom I have upheld since your birth, and have carried it since you were born. Even to your old age and gray hairs, I am he, I am he who will sustain you. I have made you and I will carry you.*
> **Isaiah 46:3-4**

In the middle of the journey to my promises, I grew more and more impatient. The last clear word the Lord had spoken to me was to wait on him. I questioned if I should stop waiting, as he encouraged me to do, and start taking action in my own hands to step into my promised land.

One night in that season, my sister had a dream about me.

"I had a dream of you as a princess driving a carriage," she said. "You were determined to get yourself to the ball. But it wasn't good! Princesses aren't supposed to drive themselves to the ball."

I knew her dream was a gentle warning to me. God was asking me to give the reins of my situation back to him—he wanted to be the one leading me. Jesus wanted to take the wheel and drive my carriage.

A few weeks later, I was leaving a conference for a lunch break when I heard the still, small voice of the Holy Spirit say, "Go and give that man selling t-shirts a prophetic word."

Uncertain if it was the voice of the Lord, I continued out the door.

"Mariel, go and speak to that man," that whisper prompted me again. I needed to obey.

"Yes, Lord," I said as I walked to the merch stand. I walked over to the man and gave him a prophetic word.

"Wait, I actually have a word for you," he said. "I see a picture of you in a carriage. Jesus is driving the carriage. He is asking you to give him the reins again."

"I know what that means," I told him.

"I thought you would," he said.

I surrendered that day. However, as more weeks went by, I wrestled again with whether I needed to take action to make my promises happen. I went to seek God again to see if he changed his mind.

I opened my Bible to a random page, and my eyes landed on the following passage: "Your carriages were heavily loaded, A burden to the weary beast" (Isaiah 46:1 NKJV).

The word "carriages" leaped off the page at me. I felt like the Holy Spirit was speaking directly to me. The written word of the Bible became a right-now rhema word—spirit and life to my soul. I continued to read the passage from Isaiah. It described how the people of Israel carried idols that became so heavy that their carriages couldn't move forward.

The Lord spoke to me, "Your carriage is stuck. You can't move forward because your promise has become a heavy idol. You've stopped trusting me to take care of you. I have carried you since you were a baby and will carry you until you are old and gray. You can trust me. Will you stop striving in your own strength? I want to drive your carriage again."

At that moment, God gave me the grace to surrender to him at a deeper level. I could trust him completely with the desires of my heart and every promise.

Bye, Bye Burden

What happens when a promise becomes a heavy burden, an idol, to us?

An idol can be anything that we put as the first priority and focus on before God. With that said, it's easy to make an idol out of lesser things in our human weakness.

This truth isn't to make us feel ashamed and condemned but to allow heart evaluation with our loving and kind King Jesus. We can respond by letting the Holy Spirit search and cleanse us.

Have we made the promise more important than the Promise Giver? If we have the conviction that we created an idol, the next step is to repent. We acknowledge our sins to God, renounce our idols, ask for forgiveness, and let the Holy Spirit renew our minds.

Then, we can invite Jesus to take the first place in our hearts again. We exchange our heavy idols for his light burden and easy yoke. We let him take the reins again.

A HEAVY CARRIAGE LOAD

> *Don't you see how wonderfully kind, tolerant, and patient God is with you? Can't you see that his kindness is intended to turn you from your sin?*
> **Romans 2:4 NLT**

When Jesus is in the driver's seat, he will get us unstuck and accelerate his plans for us.

Will you let him drive your carriage on the path to your promise?

REFLECTION

> "Come to me, all you who are weary and burdened, and I will give you rest. Take my yoke upon you and learn from me, for I am gentle and humble in heart, and you will find rest for your souls. For my yoke is easy and my burden is light."
> **Matthew 11:28-30**
>
> *Search me, God, and know my heart; test me and know my anxious thoughts. See if there is any offensive way in me, and lead me in the way everlasting.*
> **Psalm 139:23-24**

Take a moment to search your heart with the Holy Spirit. Ask the following questions and listen for his response:

- "Jesus, has a promise become an idol in my life?"
- "What does it look like for me to trust you with the promise in this season?"

If you feel led, pray the prayer of repentance below in your own words.

> *Dear Lord Jesus,*
>
> *Take the reins in my life! I choose to come to you in my weakness and lay down everything and anything I have put in the first place before you. I surrender my promise if it has become an idol, and I release it to you now. I receive your forgiveness for putting anything before you, Lord. Help me hear your voice speaking the truth over me today. Amen.*

RESTING VS. WRESTLING FOR THE PROMISE

> *The man said, "Let me go; it's daybreak."*
> *Jacob said, "I'm not letting you go 'til you bless me."*
> *The man said, "What's your name?"*
> *He answered, "Jacob."*
> *The man said, "But no longer. Your name is no longer Jacob. From now on it's Israel (God-Wrestler); you've wrestled with God and you've come through."*
> **Genesis 32:26-28 MSG**

There are times when God calls us to rest and release the promise back to him. Other times, he instructs us to wrestle and contend for the breakthrough.

We need wisdom to know when to wrestle and when to rest.

Blessing in the Wrestling

Jacob entered a wrestling match with the Angel of the Lord. When he refused to give up, God gave him a new name.

He transformed him from Jacob, which means "to deceive," to Israel, meaning "one who wrestles or struggles with God."[1]

God blessed Jacob with a new identity during their wrestling match. He was no longer a deceiver but an overcomer.

Not only that, but the angel touched Jacob's hip, giving him a limp. His struggle with God forever changed how he walked—a reminder of his divine encounter.

Like Jacob, we sometimes need to take hold of a fierce faith that declares, "God, I will not let go of you until I see the blessing you have for me!"

A blessing often awaits us on the other end of our own wrestle with Jesus. Like Israel, we will transform through the process, too.

Rhythms of Wrestle and Rest

On the pathway to the promise, we can get weary of warring—always praying and crying out for a breakthrough. We can feel like we are endlessly wrestling with God to release the blessing.

In the middle of the word *wrestle* is the word *rest*. Sometimes, we are called to wrestle for a breakthrough. Other times, we need to rest, be still, and know that God is in control. We must step into the rhythms of rest and wrestling.

How do we know what our current season requires? The answer lies in staying close to Jesus. We must continue our holy conversation with him, our Wonderful Counselor.

Our relationship with Jesus can often be like a divine dance. If we surrender to his lead, he will guide us through the choreography of the song he is currently playing in our lives. We just have to stay in step with him and lean into the rhythm of his grace.

Even in the wrestling seasons, we can learn to position ourselves from a place of rest. What would it look like to wrestle with authority, joy, and peace?

We believe with mustard-seed-size faith, knowing that he who promised is faithful. We pray with authority, knowing we are seated with Christ in heavenly places. We engage in joy and gratitude before the promise comes.

Like Jacob, we will find a blessing in the wrestling with God.

REFLECTION

> *Therefore, since the promise of entering his rest still stands, let us be careful that none of you be found to have fallen short of it.*
> **Hebrews 4:1**

Recommended Bible Reading: Genesis 32:22-32

- Do you think God has you in a rest or wrestle moment with your prophetic promise?
- Ask God, "What is my tactic for the promise in this season, wrestling or resting? How can I practically step into rest or wrestle?"

Dear Lord Jesus,

Will you show me if this is a time to rest or wrestle? If it's a time of resting, help me to place all of my cares and desires in your hands. If it's a time of wrestling, give me the strength to contend for my breakthroughs. Help me to wrestle from a place of rest and victory. Thank you for transforming me through the resting and the wrestling. Amen.

DISCERNING GOD'S VOICE

> *Do not quench the Spirit. Do not treat prophecies with contempt but test them all; hold on to what is good, reject every kind of evil.*
> **1 Thessalonians 5:19-22**

Developing the ability to hear God's voice is a journey of growth. One of the main challenges we face is distinguishing between our own thoughts and the voice of the Holy Spirit, especially when it comes to our heart's deepest desires.

Why is this such a significant challenge? Often, when we hold a specific outcome close to our hearts, we unintentionally filter God's voice through our desires. As a result, we may confuse our own thoughts with the still, small whispers of the Holy Spirit. Instead of truly hearing what God is saying, we interpret his messages based on what we want to hear. This can lead us to believe that our personal longings and preferences represent the voice of the Lord.

Our heavenly Father cares deeply about the desires of our hearts and fulfills them as we delight in him (Psalm 37:4). However, it's wise to discern between a genuine desire from the heart and a promise from God.

Jeremiah 17:9-10 cautions us that our hearts can mislead us: "The heart is deceitful above all things and beyond cure. Who can understand it? "I the Lord search the heart and examine the mind, to reward each person according to their conduct, according to what their deeds deserve."

Therefore, we must grow in the gift of discernment as we seek God's will for our lives and pursue his promises.

To authentically discern God's voice, we need to put our prophetic promises and words through a practical testing process. We can invite the Holy Spirit to examine our hearts. As the Spirit of Truth (John 16:13), he will give us wisdom and revelation, helping us to understand his will and navigate toward truth.

With that said, here are a few practical steps to test prophetic promises.

9 Steps to Test a Prophetic Promise

1. Activate Spiritual Disciplines

These disciplines will help you draw near to God and align with his heart, preparing you to hear his voice.
- **Prayer:** Ask the Holy Spirit to give you more wisdom and discernment and an open, soft heart to encounter his presence.
- **Worship:** Praise will draw you into his presence to discern his

voice and will more accurately.

- **Surrender:** Put aside your concerns, desires, distractions, and questions. Write them down if you need to get them out of your mind, then release them to God in prayer.

- **Study the Word:** Read the written word to renew your mind and heart with God's truth. Explore Bible passages that promise you the ability to hear his voice (Examples: John 10, Jeremiah 33:3, Acts 2).

- **Gratitude:** Enter God's gates with thanksgiving (Psalm 100:4). Thankfulness brings us into his presence. Make a gratitude list of all the blessings he has given you.

- **Fasting:** You may feel led to fast, which is to refrain from certain foods or activities to increase spiritual hunger and seek God. Fasting can lead to a spiritual breakthrough in discerning God's voice. (*Certain health conditions and dietary restrictions may affect fasting. Consult a physician for your specific needs.*)

2. Cultivate a Heart Attitude of Humility

"Then you will know the truth, and the truth will set you free." John 8:32

Posture your heart in humility with a mindset that says,

"Jesus, even if I am wrong and I've misheard your voice, I just want to know the truth about what I think you've promised me. I surrender my own understanding. I know you love me and have my best interest in mind, so tell me the truth regarding this area."

Additional tip: Consider bowing low on your knees before the Lord as a physical expression of humility to draw close to God.

3. Let God Search Your Heart

Invite God into conversation and bravely ask him questions, such as: "Holy Spirit, I invite you to search my heart. Have I misheard your voice? If so, what truth are you speaking to me about what you have in store for me?" and "Will you expose any areas where my heart may be deceiving me? If so, will you reveal these areas and speak truth to my heart?"

Ask more questions as you feel led. Listen for his response and journal the answers that come to your heart.

4. Weigh Words Against the Bible

Search the Bible and ask analytical questions: does this promise line up with the heart of God revealed in Scripture? Is there anything that seems out of alignment? Remove anything that does not align with God's written word.

5. Examine the Fruit

> *A good tree produces good fruit, and a bad tree produces bad fruit.* Matthew 7:17 NLT

Examine your prophetic promises and ask yourself questions. What fruit is this promise or prophetic word bearing in your life? Is it producing Galatians 5:22 fruits of the Holy Spirit in your life? Or are you finding rotten fruit? Is this process leading me into any kind of sin? Is this pursuit drawing you closer to God or away from him?

6. Test Everything and Hold Fast to the Good

> *Do not treat prophecies with contempt but test them all; hold on to what is good, reject every kind of evil.* 1 Thessalonians 5:20-22

Paul urges us to test all prophecies and hold fast to what is good.

The word "good" in this passage is translated from the Greek word *kalos*, meaning "exceedingly excellent and pleasant."[3] As you test prophetic promises and words, receive what is good. Let the Lord prune and cleanse (John 15) any areas of your promise that produce rotten fruit.

7. Receive Godly Wisdom

As iron sharpens iron, so one person sharpens another. Proverbs 27:17

Ask a few trusted and wise believers in your life to pray for you and seek God's guidance on your behalf regarding a prophetic promise or word. Find those who will pray before giving advice. Let them weigh the word against Scripture and the fruit they see in your life. Be open to feedback to help sharpen, correct, and build you up.

8. Shelf the Promise

Sometimes, you might need to completely separate yourself from the promise to gain new clarity. Take the promises and confirmations you have received and put them out of sight and mind. Rest from praying about it. Put your focus fully back on Jesus. When you start to think about it, say aloud, "I give this to you right now, Jesus."

If you put it on the shelf for a season, the Lord can bring it back to you at the right time when it is from him.

9. Trust God

Lastly, trust that God's true word will never return void. (Isa. 55:11). Sometimes, the accurate interpretation of a prophetic promise or word brings a different outcome than our initial expectations. The Lord will bring his word to fruition in his timing and way.

A word of wisdom on receiving prophetic words:

I encourage you to pray about every prophetic word and promise you receive before you accept it as truth—including words from others. Regardless of the excellent reputation or prophetically accurate track record of the one who gives you the word, nothing will replace your personal ability to hear from God. If a word does not resonate or pass the testing process, you do not have to receive it. This practice safeguards your heart from false words, manipulation, and deceptive influence. This is my charge to you to cultivate discernment and maturity in your walk with Jesus Christ.

Have I Misheard the Lord?

Give yourself grace as you grow in discerning God's voice. The Lord knows we may struggle to hear him, and he is delighted when we ask him for guidance.

Notably, Paul urged, "Do not despise prophecy." He was addressing how we can get frustrated and disillusioned as we work through the process of a prophetic promise. We can get disappointed when we find rotten fruit and false prophecies. We can question our own ability to hear God's voice accurately.

If you discern you have misheard God's voice on the journey, know that the Lord still has a beautiful plan and promises for you.

When you're ready, let Jesus heal your heart from any pain and disappointment. He will exchange your ashes for beauty and make you ready to receive a new promise from his heart. Even when prophecies seem to fail or cease, his love never fails.

> *Love never fails. But where there are prophecies, they will cease; where there are tongues, they will be stilled; where there is knowledge, it will pass away. For we know in part and we prophesy in part, but when completeness comes, what is in part disappears.*
> **1 Corinthians 13:8-10**

His love for you is immeasurable—not a single day goes by when you aren't on his mind. When he created you in your mother's womb, he designed you with a beautiful destiny in mind. Even if it seems you've misheard his voice, know there is so much in store for your future. His promises still stand. I encourage you with these words from Ephesians 2:10 (TPT):

We have become his poetry, a re-created people that will fulfill the destiny he has given each of us, for we are joined to Jesus, the Anointed One. Before we were even born, he gave us our destiny; that we would fulfill the plan of God who always accomplishes every purpose and plan in his heart.

My Prayer for You

On this journey, God will continue to refine us as he purifies the promises he has destined for us. He leads us into all truth as we come to him with humble, teachable hearts.

When you reach your promised land destination, I pray the outcome will be more than you could ever ask or dream. May Jesus exceed your expectations with what he fulfills in your life.

REFLECTION

> *For the word of God is living and active, sharper than any two-edged sword, piercing to the division of soul and of spirit, of joints and of marrow, and discerning the thoughts and intentions of the heart.*
> **Hebrews 4:12 ESV**
>
> *Let us then approach God's throne of grace with confidence, so that we may receive mercy and find grace to help us in our time of need.*
> **Hebrews 4:16**

Have you struggled to discern between your thoughts and the voice of God regarding your promise? Take time for prayer and reflection. Follow the steps above to test your prophetic words and promises. Write down your thoughts as you go through the testing process. Open your heart to recieve truth and hope from the Lord.

> *Dear Holy Spirit,*
>
> *I want to hear your voice! Please increase my discernment to know your will and heart for me above every other voice, including my own. I ask for you to clarify your promises to me again. Help me surrender anything not from you and openly receive what you have for me. Lead me into all truth, Holy Spirit of Truth! In Jesus' name, amen.*

GOD, IS THIS FROM YOU?

> *Trust in the Lord with all your heart and lean not on your own understanding; in all your ways submit to him, and he will make your paths straight.*
> **Proverbs 3:5-6**

I stood in the crystal blue-green waters of the Florida coast. Close enough to shore to walk back but far enough to be heard by anyone except God.

"Father, I am tired of this process to my promise. It's been years of following your voice, your path filled with signs and wonders. I don't want to hear anyone else's voice or opinion about my promise. Not the enemy's voice. Not the voices of people in my life. I don't even want to hear my own opinion. God, what are you truly saying about my promise?"

I left my prayer in the water and waded back to the shore. I had released my promise to God again, and this time, it felt like a burden lifted from my shoulders. Whether he confirmed my promise again or redirected me to something new, I was ready to hear the truth.

That night, God gave me a vivid dream. My prophetic promise was finally coming true. I saw a cardinal painting at my surprise engagement party. I knew instantly that the cardinal sign represented "answered prayer!" It was finally happening! And God showed me I would write a book about my story—against all opposition. I will share part two of the dream in the next chapter.

I felt renewed hope as the Lord gave me the discernment I sought. I could rest in him and take a break from asking so many questions, constantly contending for my promise. He had it in his hands—I just needed to trust and wait on him.

Release the Cardinal

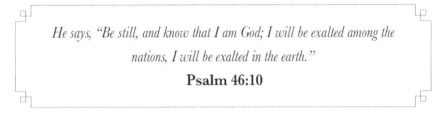

He says, "Be still, and know that I am God; I will be exalted among the nations, I will be exalted in the earth."
Psalm 46:10

Let's compare the cardinal bird to a promise from God. Could God ask you to release your cardinal—your promise—for a season?

When God asks us to release a promise, we can trust that what is meant for us will always find its way back at the right time.

I think of my first dream of the cardinal that I shared in an earlier chapter. A bright red cardinal landed on my shoulder and remained. Birds are created to be free. They are made to fly. Clinging too tightly or trying to control the things God sends never works. However, when we release the promise, the cardinal, it can freely come into our lives at the right time.

I am also reminded of the words the Holy Spirit spoke about the sign of the cardinal: "I can make all things new. I can resurrect any promise from the grave. Sometimes, you must let a bird, a promise, fly away—even die—for a season. I can always bring it back to life. Nothing is impossible for me."

What if you need to release your promise only for a season? To change, grow, and transform—so it can return at the perfect timing? What if something needs to die so God can resurrect it and transform it to be better than before in the future?

Surrender is an easy concept, but it's not always easy to practice. The act of surrendering is often as simple as a deeply heartfelt prayer to Jesus that cries, "Lord, I surrender this promise to you. I release my control. I pray for your will to be done in my life as it is in heaven, King Jesus!"

And then we genuinely take our hand off the doorknob. We release worry and embrace the peace of God and be still. We let go.

I think of the words of Jesus in Matthew 6:26-27: "Look at the birds of the air; they do not sow or reap or store away in barns, and yet your heavenly Father feeds them. Are you not much more valuable than they? Can any one of you by worrying add a single hour to your life?"

As we open our hands and release the cardinal, we can trust that the Lord will fulfill every word and promise in due time.

REFLECTION

> *At least there is hope for a tree: If it is cut down, it will sprout again, and its new shoots will not fail.*
> **Job 14:7**
>
> *Very truly I tell you, unless a kernel of wheat falls to the ground and dies, it remains only a single seed. But if it dies, it produces many seeds.*
> **John 12:24**

- Take a moment and reflect. Has God prompted you to open your hands and release a promise? Is he prompting you to let go today?

- If you feel like God is prompting you to open your hands and let go of the promise for a season, you can pray the prayer below.

Dear Heavenly Father,

I surrender! I choose to open my hands and let go today, Lord. I trust the promise is now held safely in your hands. Transform my promise, God, to be ready for me at the right time. Resurrect it to be better than before. Thank you for bringing back what you sent in your perfect time. I will be still and know you are God. In Jesus' name, amen.

WARFARE AT THE DOOR OF DESTINY

> *Put on the full armor of God, so that you can take your stand against the devil's schemes.*
> **Ephesians 6:11**

My dream about my surprise engagement party suddenly switched to a new scene.

I saw a close-up image of the hinge of a door, and a tiny black widow spider appeared on it. I looked closer, and a second one popped up. I jumped back in fear. Suddenly, the Father came to my rescue and destroyed the insects with a spray. I felt a sense of relief as the dream ended.

Through part two of the dream, God exposed what was happening behind the scenes of my promise. He revealed to me that the spiders represented demonic forces trying to steal and destroy my hope by weaving webs of lies of unbelief.

I learned that the word "cardinal" comes from the Latin word *cardo*, which has a root word that means "hinge," specifically the pivot point on which a door swings.³ Therefore, the hinge of the door in the dream represented my cardinal, my answered prayer.

The thief tried to ruin my promises with lies of hopelessness and unbelief, but even if there were attempted attacks, no weapon formed against me, or my answered prayers would prosper. By killing the spiders in my dream, my heavenly Father was showing me he was on the defense. He was going to take care of my enemies.

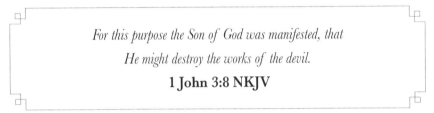

For this purpose the Son of God was manifested, that He might destroy the works of the devil.
1 John 3:8 NKJV

Threshold of Promise

The enemy often wages war at the doorway to our destiny. His aim is to keep us from crossing the threshold to our promised land. We do not need to be intimidated by his tactics. In fact, I don't like to give too much attention or credit to the enemy. Jesus Christ is more powerful than any spiritual warfare we face.

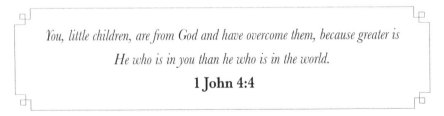

You, little children, are from God and have overcome them, because greater is He who is in you than he who is in the world.
1 John 4:4

When God exposes the works of the enemy in our life, like in my dream, it gives us victory to overcome. We now have greater discernment to know how to pray with greater power.

The Hebrew word for "intercession" is *paga* (פָּגַע), which means "to strike the target" or "to meet."[4] When we intercede according to God's spiritual strategies, we meet the problem at the root and strike the target in prayer until a breakthrough comes.

When we begin to pray with authority and discernment by what God has shown us prophetically through dreams, visions, signs, and wonders, we engage in the powerful warfare tool of *prophetic intercession*. This area is what those carrying prophetic promises excel in most.

We are called to rise up in our spiritual authority, bind the enemy, and destroy the works of the devil. We have this kind of power not by our own righteousness but through the blood and righteousness of our Lord and Savior, Jesus Christ.

If warfare is raging against your promises, it must mean that a major heavenly turnaround is ahead. You can take heart that your promise is going to advance the kingdom of God and make the darkness run. Hell is afraid of you and the glory your testimony of God's faithfulness carries. And when you overcome the warfare against you, you will recieve an anointing to help others get set free and step into victory, too. The enemy will regret the day he messed with God's chosen ones.

Pray for the Lord to expose and remove the enemy's assignment and for your promises to be realized. Like the hinge of a door, our prayers are pivotal to seeing the door of promise open.

Don't give up before the breakthrough—fight the good fight by continuing to prophesy and pray your prophetic promises until you hear the sound of the hinge of the door swinging wide open.

REFLECTION

> *"I have given you authority to trample on snakes and scorpions and to overcome all the power of the enemy; nothing will harm you."*
> **Luke 10:19**
>
> *Because he loves Me, I will deliver him; because he knows My name, I will protect him. When he calls out to Me, I will answer him; I will be with him in trouble.* **Psalm 91:14-15**

Recommended Bible Reading: Ephesians 6, Psalm 91

Prophetic Activation: Have you faced unusual spiritual warfare on the path to your promises? Pray and ask God the following questions and journal his response.

- "Holy Spirit, will you show me what the enemy doesn't want me to see? Will you reveal to me why spiritual warfare has come against me, and how I can victoriously overcome it?"

- "Father God, will you give me Bible promises to declare and stand on until I see breakthrough and victory?"

- "Lord Jesus, will you show me a picture of how you are defeating my enemies?"

Dear Lord Jesus,

Thank you for giving victory by the power of your blood! Thank you for exposing and destroying all of the work of the enemy coming against me and those I love. Shut every door I have opened, knowingly or unaware, to the enemy's schemes. Give me supernatural strategies to overcome. I declare Psalm 91 over me and my promised land—you will deliver me from all power of the enemy and bring every promise to pass! Amen.

2222: DOORS OF DESTINY

> *I will place on his shoulder the key to the house of David; what he opens no one can shut, and what he shuts no one can open.*
> **Isaiah 22:22**

In my own process to the promise, God has often used the metaphor of opening and closing doors in my life. Doors can represent all kinds of opportunities and options presented to us.

As I have asked Jesus to direct me, he has sent many people out of the blue to pray for me from Isaiah 22:22: "Dear Lord, thank you for shutting the wrong doors and opening the right ones in Mariel's life!"

Whether it's a friend or a stranger, in the form of a voicemail or altar call prayer, people have prayed this for me many times over the years. This typically happens when God wants to shut a door in my life—and he does so quickly.

The truth is that we will be offered many doors in different seasons. We need discernment to know which doorways to walk through.

Just because an open door appears good doesn't mean it is God-sent. Maybe it's not a bad door—it's just not his best for you.

Our God-ordained doors may be few and far between—but they are life-changing destiny doors. These thresholds are worth waiting for.

That is why Isaiah 22:22 is such a powerful Scripture to pray. It helps to align us with God's will and timing and can increase our spiritual discernment when making decisions. It helps us to trust Jesus when he shuts a door. It gives us confidence to walk through a door he opens. And many times, a door must shut before a new one opens.

Maybe a God door was opened for a time, but now it must be barred shut for your new season. Your next door of destiny will open at the right time.

Now, whenever I see the number 2222, I am reminded of the power in praying Isaiah 22:22.

God is an excellent Doorkeeper, and I can trust him to do his job better than I can.

A Wide-Open Door

> *I know your deeds. See, I have placed before you an open door that no one can shut. I know that you have little strength, yet you have kept my word and have not denied my name.*
> **Revelation 3:8**

During a season of transition, I started seeking God for my next steps. I had been living at home for about a year after finishing ministry school, working as a nanny. I felt in my heart that a significant change was right around the corner.

To prepare, I began to increase my prayer life by praying Isaiah 22:22 as often as possible while also praying in the spirit.

I started planning to move to Atlanta to pursue a career in film. I found a house to rent with three good friends—it seemed like the perfect opportunity.

A few days after signing the lease, a new friend invited me to a revival event in their city. I typed in the location, and it was precisely 2 hours and 22 minutes from my address.

While driving to the revival, I saw the car's license plate in front of me with 2222 on it. I looked over, and there was a truck with the numbers 222-2222 on the side of it. Directly above it, I saw a billboard with the phone number 222-2222.

It seemed like a convergence of God's signs confirming my Isaiah 22:22 prayer—he was opening the right doors and shutting the wrong ones in my life.

I had a great time at the revival. Many people were saved, healed, and delivered at the event. It was powerful! I enjoyed exploring a new city and made several new friends.

Right before I left to head home, I got a phone call from one of the girls I was supposed to move in with. They told me the lease had fallen through on the house, and they had already found another place to live … without me. The door slammed shut.

I had been praying so much that I was not upset when they told me the news. I knew God must have a different plan for me.

When I returned home, I continued to pray about my next step.

As I cleaned my room one day, I heard a voice say, "Behold!"

I looked around, startled. The voice continued, "This will be a sign to you: when the woman you're nannying for is pregnant, your job with them will be done."

Did I just make that up? I thought to myself. *I probably made that up! If I didn't, the woman I am nannying for has been struggling with infertility. What if that means I have to stay at this job for a few more years? That probably wasn't God...*

I brushed off the thought and forgot about it for the rest of the day.

When I arrived at my nanny job the next morning, the mother sat me down.

"Mariel, we don't need you to nanny for us anymore. I am pregnant with twins. I am going to quit my job and be a stay-at-home mom," she said.

She slid the black and white pictures of the ultrasounds across the kitchen room table to me. As I looked at the photos in disbelief, she grabbed her keys and rushed out the door to work.

An hour later, Ellen, one of the leaders of the revival event, called me and asked if I needed a job. I was stunned. I told her I had just lost my job and would be happy to move and work for the ministry for the summer.

Door of Destiny

A few months later, the leaders of that ministry invited me to teach on the prophetic gift for an evangelism conference in a small town in Alabama. As we drove to the event, I fell asleep and had a dream.

I saw a door an inch from my face when it suddenly flung up. I was so close to the door, and it felt so real that I awoke with a start.

I heard the Lord say, "I am opening the door of opportunity to launch you into prophetic ministry."

That trip was the first of many opportunities I would take with that ministry for the next two years. God opened the door to help me step into my calling to teach on the prophetic gift at different churches around the United States and Canada. These opportunities would set a solid foundation for starting my own ministry one day.

When we take our hands off the doorknob and trust God to shut the wrong doors in our lives, he is faithful to open destiny doors at the right time. In fact, he is not only a doorkeeper, but also the Door (John 10:7). Keep following Jesus, and he will open every door on the path to your promises.

REFLECTION

> *So Jesus again said to them, "Truly, truly, I say to you, I am the door of the sheep. All who came before me are thieves and robbers, but the sheep did not listen to them. I am the door. If anyone enters by me, he will be saved and will go in and out and find pasture."*
> **John 10:7-9 ESV**

Recommended Bible Reading: John 10:1-18

- Has God opened a door for you that couldn't open on your own?
- When has he shut a door in your life?
- Pray and ask the Lord, "Jesus, will you give me wisdom and revelation on why these doors have shut and opened in my life?"

Dear Lord Jesus,

Will you be a Doorkeeper in my life? I take my hand off the doorknob and invite you to shut the wrong doors in my life and open the right ones according to Isaiah 22:22 and Revelation 3:7. Help me to trust you when the door slams shut. You know what is best for me, and at the right time, I pray for you to open my destiny doors! Amen.

BECOME A LIVING SACRIFICE

> *Therefore, I urge you, brothers and sisters, in view of God's mercy, to offer your bodies as a living sacrifice, holy and pleasing to God—this is your true and proper worship. Do not conform to the pattern of this world, but be transformed by the renewing of your mind. Then you will be able to test and approve what God's will is—his good, pleasing and perfect will.*
> **Romans 12:1-2**

On this path to the promise, we have an invitation to let our lives become a living, burning sacrifice that cries, "Not my will, but yours be done, Lord Jesus!"

What does it look like to become a living sacrifice to God?

It looks like obeying him no matter the cost.

It looks like letting go when he asks us to open our hands and trust him.

It looks like worshiping him through every test, trial, and turn of this life.

It looks like choosing his will again and again and again—even when it can seem tempting to forge our own path without him.

This kind of submission to God's ways can be painfully difficult at times. But a fully surrendered heart is a beautiful, pleasing sacrifice to Jesus. It is fragrant worship we can only offer on this side of Heaven.

Giving Jesus all of our lives is like spilling perfume worth an annual salary at his feet. Others may see it as a waste, but it moves God's heart.

This is a costly perfume we carry, and it often pours out once the alabaster box of our hearts break open. To become a fragrant offering, the oil, the perfume, we often go through a crushing process. A crushing happens each time we surrender our will for God's will. While the process may be painful, Jesus is so worthy of it all.

The beautiful thing is God's will for us is so much better tailored to our life than our own plans. After all, our heavenly Father created us with the dreams and desires of our hearts. He knows us better than we know ourselves.

When he asks us to follow him and lay down our will in exchange for his, we can trust he always has a good plan waiting for us up ahead. As Jesus said in Matthew 16:25, "For whoever wants to save their life will lose it, but whoever loses their life for me will find it."

Choosing a God-promise means choosing a God-plan to reach it. His narrow path may be marked with testing, refining, purification, and surrender. It may require us to lay our plans and promises on the altar, time and time again.

It's not an easy road. That's why many people don't choose this way. But it is more than worth it. God will make the pain worth it. He is preparing your tests to become testimonies of his goodness, grace, and glory.

In this process, God desires to complete an extraordinary work in your heart. He is not just on a mission to fulfill what he spoke to you—he is focused on another chief goal.

Through the fires of testing, he's making you ready for what he promised you.

You will make it out on the other side of the refiner's fire.

And when his work is finished, you will come forth as gold.

REFLECTION

For we are the aroma of Christ to God among those who are being saved and among those who are perishing, to one a fragrance from death to death, to the other a fragrance from life to life.
2 Corinthians 2:15-16 ESV

Not only so, but we also glory in our sufferings, because we know that suffering produces perseverance; perseverance, character; and character, hope. And hope does not put us to shame, because God's love has been poured out into our hearts through the Holy Spirit, who has been given to us.
Romans 5:3-5

Dear Lord Jesus,

You are worthy of my whole life laid down at your feet. Give me the grace to surrender to you when you ask me. I want to be a living, burning sacrifice that worships you with everything I have, holding nothing back. Let my surrender on the altar become worship—a sweet fragrance—to you! Amen.

PROPHETIC ENCOURAGEMENT
FOURTH MAN IN THE FIRE

> *He said, "Look! I see four men walking around in the fire, unbound and unharmed, and the fourth looks like a son of the gods."*
> **Daniel 3:25**

You may feel like you are in the refiner's fire of testing. Hold on a little bit longer. It's not the end of the story.

I heard the Lord say, "I am the fourth man in the fire with you. I have never left you alone, not even for a moment. In the flames of testing, your faith is being proved as genuine. You are coming out of the fire as pure as gold.

When you emerge, you will be amazed at your transformation. What didn't destroy you truly made you stronger. You will not even smell like the smoke of your fiery trial. You will not carry the residue of the trauma of the past season on the other side of the furnace. In fact, you will release the scent of fragrant worship, like the Rose of Sharon. Your life will be a supernatural fragrance of my grace and mercy everywhere you go.

Your enemies will tremble when they see you because it will be evident that I am on your side. What looked like your downfall was your most significant promotion. The heat only fortified your purpose. The fire only launched you deeper into your destiny.

Do not look back at the ashes of what burned down around you— all of the things that the fire took. The past is gone. Instead, gaze into my eyes of fire, passionate for you.

> *His eyes are like blazing fire, and on his head are many crowns.*
> **Revelation 19:12**

As you behold me, the smoke will clear. You will catch a new vision for the beautiful beginning I have for you. You are called to a high calling, and the refining fire prepares you for it. Testing comes before promotion—so be ready to walk into higher levels of your calling.

> *Consider it pure joy, my brothers and sisters, whenever you face trials of many kinds, because you know that the testing of your faith produces perseverance. Let perseverance finish its work so that you may be mature and complete, not lacking anything.* **James 1:2-4**

Your refining moment is becoming your defining moment. You are arising from your test with a testimony full of my goodness and glory. You are coming out of the flames as pure as gold."

PART 7
ENTER THE PROMISED LAND

AND SO THE ADVENTURE BEGINS

The time has finally come—your long-awaited moment is at hand.

Your promised land is closer than you ever imagined.

After the long journey,

You can hear the sound of the Jordan River rushing in the distance.

You can see new land coming into view.

This is not a mirage.

The chapter of your wilderness wandering is ending.

God is calling you forward.

He is calling you to step into your promises.

POMEGRANATES OF PROMISE

> *For the Lord your God is bringing you into a good land—a land with brooks, streams, and deep springs gushing out into the valleys and hills; a land with wheat and barley, vines and fig trees, pomegranates, olive oil and honey; a land where bread will not be scarce and you will lack nothing.*
> **Deuteronomy 8:7-9**

One night in August of 2020, I had a dream from God I will never forget.

At midnight, a friend picked me up from my house in her Jeep. Windows down, I rode in the passenger seat as she drove us to some unknown destination. I remember feeling a cool breeze as we moved through the night, so tangible it felt like it wasn't a dream. I felt carefree and content—the opposite of how I felt in my waking life.

In reality, I felt deeply hopeless. After years of praying for my promises to come to pass, I saw no signs of a breakthrough. Yet, God kept leading me to believe he wasn't finished with my promises. He kept confirming his word to me through consistent signs and wonders. After years of my journey, I was tired of contending in faith and staying on his narrow path. I felt like giving up for the thousandth time.

Then, I had this dream ...

Suddenly, I realized my friend had driven us to a graveyard with just enough dim moonlight from the moon and stars to see around us. She parked the Jeep on top of a tombstone. Something caught my eye in front of the grave. This was the reason she brought me here.

Peering through the twilight, I saw a bush full of fruit growing from the grave, gently rustling in the breeze. I drew in for a closer look. The fruit was unlike anything I had ever seen—it was shaped like a simple crown as if a child had designed it. It glowed in the dark.

"This is exactly what I wanted!" I said as tears welled up in my eyes. I felt a deep sense of wonder and gratitude in my heart. However, in my natural mind, I didn't understand why the fruit was so meaningful to me. *Why was I moved to tears?*

Then, the scene switched in the dream, and I saw the fruit served on a table for Thanksgiving.

I woke up from the dream, amazed.

Not every dream is from God, but as you walk with the Holy Spirit, you can grow in the gift of discernment and interpretation to understand the messages God is giving in the night seasons. This was no ordinary dream. I knew God had just spoken to me.

If God was speaking, what was he saying?

I Spy

Later that day, as I stepped out the door to take my dog, Sebastian, on a walk, something caught my eye in the distant field across the street.

Are those bushes full of ... fruit? I thought to myself.

My heart began to pound with excitement as I went to explore.

I was visiting my mother that week; she had lived across from this field for over twelve years. It belonged to a church, and I had gone on many prayer walks talking to Jesus there over the years.

The bushes had never borne fruit to my knowledge ... until now.

As I drew nearer, I saw more clearly.

Pomegranates. The two bushes were full of pomegranates. At least *twenty* of them!

I picked one and saw a crown shape adorning it—exactly like the crown from my dream.

Waves of wonder and awe surged through me. Jesus was showing me a sign to confirm the dream he had given me.

You may find this funny, but pomegranates were unfamiliar to me—I had never even bought one from the grocery store! I didn't think to relate the crown-shaped fruit from the dream to the pomegranate until that moment.

Tears fill my eyes as I write this, and I remember how I felt when God spoke a mystery to me in that field. From that day on, God began to reveal the prophetic meaning he had for me through the pomegranate.

The Prophetic Sign of the Pomegranate

I want to give you a sneak peek into my process of interpreting my dream from God.

When it comes to dream interpretation from a Christian perspective, the best place to start to understand a dream is—you may have guessed it—the Bible. As I began to research the meaning of the pomegranate, I found that it was an important symbol in the Bible and Jewish Tradition, signifying to me that it was a treasure to seek out. Here are a few keys that I discovered.

Pomegranates in the Bible and Jewish Tradition

- The Hebrew word for pomegranate is "rimmon" (רִמּוֹן). It contains the root word raman, meaning "to be exalted" or "to be lifted up."[1]

- In Exodus, God commands skilled workers to embroider blue, purple, and scarlet pomegranates with golden bells between them on the hem of the priestly robes (Ex. 28:33-35).

- Solomon decorated the pillars of the temple with bronze pomegranates (2 Chron. 3:16).

- In the Song of Solomon, pomegranates represent the passionate love of the bridegroom for his bride (Song 4:13, 6:11).

- Pomegranates were one of the fruits of the Promised Land (Deut. 8:8).

- During the Jewish feast of Rosh Hashanah, otherwise known as the Feast of Trumpets, pomegranates are served on the second night as a symbolic act of believing God for a fruitful and blessed new year.[2]

- In Jewish tradition, pomegranates are thought to have 613 seeds to represent the 613 laws of the Torah (however, the true number of seeds varies by pomegranate.)[3]

As I sought out the meaning of the dream, God began to speak to me a prophetic message not just for me but for his people in the times and seasons we are living in.

Dream Interpretation

Let's break down the dream by setting, timing, symbols, and themes to arrive at a prophetic message.

Time: Midnight

The dream occurred at midnight—symbolizing the last and darkest hour of the day when time has run out.

Place: Graveyard

It took place in a graveyard because I felt like my promise from God was sleeping in the grave—dead, with no signs of life or movement.

Significant Symbols: Pomegranates

The crowned fruit represented the pomegranate—the fruit of the Promised Land, the word of God, and intimacy with Jesus. It symbolizes God's beautiful word and promises fulfilled.

Fruit at the Grave

The fruit bush grew from the grave because God's promises were still alive and active through his resurrection power. The fruit glowed in the dark because God's promises can be seen even in the darkest hour.

Themes: Desires Fulfilled

I was moved to tears when I saw the glowing fruit because it represented the fruit of promises fulfilled. It was "exactly what I wanted" because it was a sign of John 15 fruit:

> *If you abide in me, and my words abide in you, ask whatever you wish, and it will be done for you. By this my Father is glorified, that you bear much fruit and so prove to be my disciples.*
> **John 15:7-8**

As I continued to abide in Jesus and pray through the years of my difficult faith journey, he was bearing good fruit in my life—the fruit of desires fulfilled.

Thanksgiving

The dream ended with the fruit being served at Thanksgiving. There was coming a day when the fruit would be harvested to be enjoyed with gratitude to God for what he has done. The promises would be fulfilled.

Timing of the Dream in Waking Life: I had the dream a few weeks before Rosh Hashanah. As I mentioned previously, pomegranates are a part of the head of the year celebration and represent believing for new and unusual fruit. God was speaking a word not just for a new year but for the new era that the church was entering into.

The Promised Land is Ahead

I believe finding the pomegranate bush in full bloom after my dream meant that I was spying on the fruit of the promised land for God's people, like Joshua and Caleb. God's promises were up ahead—

nearer now than ever before.

Many have spent years wandering wildernesses and pruning seasons, waiting for God's word to come to pass in their lives. We can feel like we are in an endless waiting room for a promise far past its due date, having taken every step of obedience and faith we know to take, only to be left wondering, *Where is the fulfillment of the promise? Will it ever happen?*

But God does not make a promise without bringing it to pass. Even promises that seem dead in the grave will experience the resurrection power of Christ at the midnight hour.

God is a miracle worker, after all.

As sure as the pomegranates bloomed and glowed in the dark, his promises are alive and active in the darkest night, in the final hour.

We are living in an Isaiah 60 era. Although there is a deep darkness covering the earth, God's glory will shine through our lives as he bears the beautiful fruit of promise in our lives. When we submit to his will in his way, we get his fruitful results. We will see many long-awaited promises of God unfold with our own eyes.

I spied the pomegranate of promise.

It was not just a sign for me but a prophetic promise for the body of Christ.

It was time to prepare to enter the promised land.

PROPHETIC ENCOURAGEMENT
THE FRUIT OF PROMISE IS COMING

I heard the Lord say, "The fruit of your promised land is coming. My word will not return void. Your obedience and labor were not in vain. I have seen your faithfulness to follow me—not loving your life unto death. You have chosen to obey me no matter the cost. Even the promises that seem lifeless in the grave will experience my resurrection power at the midnight hour. The appointed time is coming that you will finally taste and see—fully experience—the fruit of promise blooming in your life."

REFLECTION

> *Is there yet any seed left in the barn? Until now, the vine and the fig tree, the pomegranate and the olive tree have not borne fruit.*
>
> *"'From this day on I will bless you.'"*
>
> **Haggai 2:19**
>
> *I went down to the grove of nut trees to look at the new growth in the valley, to see if the vines had budded or the pomegranates were in bloom.*
>
> **Song of songs 6:11**

- What is your pomegranate of promise from God?
- What signs and confirmations has God given you of your promised land ahead?

Dear Lord Jesus,

I pray for eyes of faith to see what you are doing in the dark midnight hour of my life. Thank you that your promises are alive and active, even in the valley of dry bones. I pray for your resurrection power to touch the promises of my life that seem dead in the grave. I declare that nothing is too hard for you! I give you praise in advance because I believe I have spied the promise, and my fulfillment is coming to the glory of God! Amen.

GOD'S GOOD REPORT

> *They gave Moses this account: "We went into the land to which you sent us, and it does flow with milk and honey! Here is its fruit."*
> **Numbers 13:27**

When you spy the pomegranates of promise, you must wholeheartedly believe God's good report. It's time to go in and conquer the land.

When Moses sent Caleb, Joshua, and the other ten spies to search out the promised land, he said to them, "Be of good courage and bring some of the fruit of the land" (Num. 13:20).

So, Caleb, Joshua, and the spies did exactly that.

In Numbers 12:23, it says, "'And they came to the Valley of Eshcol and cut down from there a branch with a single cluster of grapes, and they carried it on a pole between two of them; they also brought some pomegranates and figs."

As you just read, the twelve spies brought pomegranates when they returned from Canaan. The fruit was a physical sign of God's promise. Yet, they also brought news of giants in the land.

When you hear the report of the pomegranates of promise, you don't have to listen to the rumors of giants or the unbelieving complaints of the majority. You can step in and take your promised land. Why? Because God said so. Period.

Pomegranate Gifts

A few months after my pomegranate dream, God gave me a supernatural confirmation about its prophetic meaning. I was at the altar at the end of a church service, on my knees before the Lord. A lady knelt beside me and began to pray for me. As she prayed, the Holy Spirit whispered, "Tell her what I've been teaching you about the pomegranates."

When it was my turn to pray for her, I said, "Lord, thank you for fulfilling her long-awaited promises, like you've been showing me about the meaning of the pomegranate."

She burst into tears and joyful laughter. I continued praying for her and told her what God showed me about Rosh Hashanah and the sign of the pomegranate.

When I finished praying, she said, "I am amazed by God! I have Jewish roots, so I understood what you said about the pomegranate and Rosh Hashanah. Over the last few months, people have randomly given me pomegranates as gifts. I even received a basket full of them! Yesterday, I found a pomegranate outside on my doorstep. I had no idea where it came from. I felt it was a sign from God, but I didn't know what it meant. I have been praying about marrying a man who wants to propose to me. I have been married before, and I told God I do not want to get married again unless it is his plan. Everything you just prayed for me shows me what he was saying about the pomegranate. This is confirmation of my long-awaited promise of re-marriage."

The prophetic word she received gave her assurance and joy in believing God's good report for her life. I was just as encouraged as my new friend. When God encounters someone through you, it fills you with faith, too.

Your Choice

The pomegranate is the invitation to believe the good report. When we hear the news of the land ahead and its obstacles, we can look behind us and long to return to the predictable manna and the quail in the wilderness. We may even desire to go back to the familiar slavery of Egypt. Or, we can choose to embark on the new and unknown path where God is leading us.

Possessing God's promises will require:

- Belief in the good report over the negative report
- Deeper trust in God to help you cross over into the new
- Leaving the familiarity of the past for a new season
- Courage to move into unknown territory

The promised land is ahead, my friend. When you hear the report of the promise, what will you choose?

REFLECTION

> *Then Caleb silenced the people before Moses and said, "We should go up and take possession of the land, for we can certainly do it."*
> **Numbers 13:30**

Recommended Bible Reading: Numbers 13-14

- Are you hearing a negative report about your promises? What is it? Is it coming from your own thoughts, someone in your life, or the enemy?

- Ask Jesus, "What positive report are you giving today about what you've promised me?" Journal the words and scriptures God brings to your heart.

Dear Heavenly Father,

I choose to believe your good report about my promises! I reject every negative report. I will stand on your word even when I face opposition, doubt, and unbelief. Nothing is impossible for you! I declare I will step into my promised land! In Jesus' name, amen.

RUMORS OF GIANTS

> *"There we saw the giants (the descendants of Anak came from the giants); and we were like grasshoppers in our own sight, and so we were in their sight."*
> **Numbers 13:33 NKJV**

When we hear the rumors of giants in the land, will we be filled with worry or wonder?

Ten of the twelve fearful spies spread the rumor that entering Canaan was dangerous. Despite God's encouragement, the negative report declared that the Israelites were like small bugs in the eyes of their enemies.

Out of fear and unbelief, the people of Israel chose to believe the negative report over God's promises. The journey out of the wilderness could have taken them a quick eleven days. Yet, they chose to stay back and wandered in the wilderness for another forty years! They forfeited the promise to the next generation.

When an obstacle too big for us arises, blocking the path of promise, we can take it as a sign that we are positioned for an incredible miracle. We can't take the land without God's help—but he wouldn't have it any other way. Didn't we learn dependence on his power and provision in the wilderness of wonders?

It's time to embrace child-like faith, wonder, and trust as we enter the land of promise and conquer the giants.

Mega Bugs

I felt like Jesus was calling me to go to the local gardens during Good Friday. I planned on going—but then I changed my mind.

Travel forty minutes outside of town with a headache? I thought to myself. *I better stick to the local coffee shop today.*

I was crossing the 13th Street bridge when the thought crossed my mind: *I wonder if I should go anyway...*

I looked up just in time to see a digital billboard change to an ad for the local gardens.

"You should go," that still small voice of the Holy Spirit gently prompted me. So, I changed my route and headed to the gardens.

Earlier that week, I saw a vision of myself sitting in the garden chapel. Stained glass windows shone around me, casting colors of orange, red, and yellow. I felt the Holy Spirit compelling me to go and meet with him there.

The next day, I woke up from another vision. I was standing beside a giant praying mantis—taller than me! Unusual. I didn't know if I was somehow making the image up or if it was from God. I felt foolish writing it down, but I did anyway. I've learned it's better to record than to ignore potential Holy Spirit signs.

As I drove, I pondered the visions. The praying mantis had become a sign of praying and prophesying God's promises. But I was tired of believing for my breakthrough.

How do you keep hoping when so much time has passed, and you haven't seen the promises come true? I've stopped counting all of the times I've asked God to redirect me if I'm wrong about his word to me. I just want to know if I am following the wrong path and if the signs don't mean what I think they mean.

Yet, I know that even in my wondering that Jesus always meets me. He is a man of sorrows, well-acquainted with grief. He understands the depth of my pain and longsuffering in the mysterious process. He is a one-of-a-kind friend.

In the waiting for my promises, what if this despair I feel is a piece of what the Bride is supposed to feel for the return of our Bridegroom Jesus—the greatest prophetic promise yet to be fulfilled? A hope and a longing so great she can hardly stand it that she doesn't know when her Bridegroom will come for her? What if I am experiencing an anguish of intercession for his return that I am living out prophetically through my own story?

This process is stretching the little faith clinging alive inside of me. Jesus asked in a parable, 'When the son of man comes, will he find faith on the earth?' (Luke 18:8) How do I have faith that endures?

Yet, when I think about the trail of signs and wonders, the tender voice of my Good Shepherd leading me forward, I can't help but keep believing he is not finished yet ... even if all I have is faith the size of a tiny mustard seed. When I remember my history with Jesus, I don't want another plan—I want his plan. I want what he has promised me.

RUMORS OF GIANTS

When I drove into the gardens, the woman at the park kiosk gave me a map. I looked at it, and the first thing I saw shocked me. A giant cartoon praying mantis smiled back at me from the map. The description next to it said, "MEGA BUGS."

When I saw the word "MEGA," I knew it was an obvious sign. I was about to discover a giant praying mantis the day after I had a vision of one.

My adventure began. I went on a search to find the MEGA BUGS area at the kids' park discovery zone.

I knew I arrived at the right place when I spotted a massive centipede. Then, giant ladybugs. A colossal grasshopper. *It must be here*, I thought to myself, my heart pounding.

Then I saw it—a huge pink orchid towering toward the sky, and beneath it, a giant pink and green praying mantis. Taller than a human. It was a sight to behold.

I took in the wonder and reminded myself this was not a coincidence. I hear God.

What do you do when a sign becomes a wonder? You pray. What else is there to do?

I prayed as I walked. I passed bumble bees, scorpions, and katydids. I declared the promises of God in faith as I observed the mega bugs surrounding me.

I couldn't help but relate the giant praying mantis to a sign of the promised land. After all, the spies said they were "like grasshoppers in the sight of the giants" (Num. 13:33). I felt pretty small standing next to a giant grasshopper-like bug, hovering over me.

I heard the Lord say, "Mariel, this is a sign and wonder. You have not misheard my voice. You saw this giant praying mantis in a vision, and then it came to pass in real life. I am encouraging you to keep believing for the promises I've shown you. They're coming. Do not be intimidated by the giants on the way to your promised land—continue to pray and prophesy my promises. In the same way you have found this sign in a children's play area, I am calling you to keep having child-like faith for the impossible. Believe my good report. It's time to prepare to go in and take the promised land I have for you."

If God had to say the same thing to me in one thousand different ways to keep me on the pathway to his promises, he would go to every length—even if that meant sending the sign of the praying mantis—praying prophet—in unusual ways.

I am called to be one that keeps praying and prophesying until I see the prophetic promise with my own eyes—and to champion others as they do the same.

Mustard-Seed-Size Faith

> *"Truly I tell you, if you have faith as small as a mustard seed, you can say to this mountain, 'Move from here to there,' and it will move. Nothing will be impossible for you."*
> **Matthew 17:20**

Will you continue to pray and prophesy God's promises, no matter what comes your way and no matter how long it takes? Will you believe that he wants to answer your prayers and fulfill his word?

God is calling his people to have enduring, mustard-seed-sized faith on this path to his promises. It's time for God's praying mantises—praying prophets—to rise up and take the land.

REFLECTION

> *For in this hope we were saved. But hope that is seen is no hope at all. Who hopes for what they already have?*
> **Romans 8:24**

- Have you grown weary of believing for the promise?
- Ask Jesus, "Lord, will you remind me of what you've spoken?
- "Will you encourage my heart with a new word today?" Listen for his response and write it down.

Dear Lord Jesus,

I pray for enduring faith! Give me the fortitude to continue to pray and prophesy your promises until I see the answer. Thank you for helping me to overcome every giant, mountain, and obstacle in my way. I declare they are coming down at your name! Increase my faith to cross the threshold to my inheritance. Amen.

EMBOLDENED

> *"Have I not commanded you? Be strong and courageous. Do not be afraid; do not be discouraged, for the LORD your God will be with you wherever you go."*
> **Joshua 1:9**

In Joshua chapter one, it's finally time for God's people to enter the Promised Land.

After the children of Israel wandered in the desert for forty years, everything was about to change in a few days' journey. They are going somewhere they've never been before, where they will face daunting obstacles and challenges. They must be brave.

When God calls Joshua to advance into Canaan, he doesn't tell him to *feel* courageous—he *commands* him to be brave. You, too, need great courage as you forge ahead into your promises.

When Jesus asks us to leave our comfort zones for an unfamiliar territory, it's normal to feel afraid. It's pivotal transitions like this that bravery must become an action, not an emotion.

Choosing courage doesn't mean you won't feel the emotion of fear; it means you take a bold leap forward anyway. God wants to expand your territory, and your calling requires you to venture into the unknown. Where he is taking you is much greater than what you are leaving behind—a land flowing with milk and honey. Resolve in your heart to choose faith over fear.

Wild Leap

> *For we walk by faith, not by sight.* **2 Corinthians 5:7 ESV**

God, is it time for me to leave my wilderness yet?

I was having a tough day at my 9-5 job and dreamed of finding another position. I knew the Lord had placed me in this role for a season, but I hadn't yet sensed a grace to leave. Regardless, I quickly searched LinkedIn and applied for a random position at a church planting company in a different city. I wasn't seriously looking for another job, but it felt like an act of faith to submit my resume. I needed a glimmer of hope that I wasn't stuck at my current job forever.

That same night, I had a simple dream. I saw my LinkedIn inbox with a new message notification about the job I had applied to. I woke up afraid. I had an intuitive feeling that the dream was literal. Sure enough, I went to check my inbox, and there was a message from the company asking to set up an interview with me. I wasn't ready to leave my current job—especially if I had to move to another city! I brushed the idea off.

Later that week, I woke up from sleep to the voice of the Lord, like a surround sound speaker in my room, "I pray you would take the leap of faith and take the job!"

Was Jesus telling me this random job was actually his plan for me? I hadn't even interviewed for the position yet! In faith, I went into the job interview anyway. During the process, I told them I am a writer with skills in copywriting. They left the room for a moment and returned with a new application.

"We don't think you're the right fit for the position you applied for," the manager said. "But we just had the job for our writer open up today if you want to apply for that role instead."

I agreed to re-apply—shocked that a better-fitting role opened up that same day. As I drove home from the interview, I saw a giant billboard that said, "WILD LEAP!"

During my lunch break the next day, I went into a boutique, and the first thing I saw was a silver and gold bracelet with a label next to it that said *Leap of Faith*. I bought the bracelet. I was still afraid about making a major life change, but I was encouraged by how sweetly and clearly God confirmed his word to me.

The week of my interview, the 2020 shutdown commenced. Everything stopped with the job hiring process. I began to have recurring dreams that I was getting a new job but still living in my current city. I didn't understand—the dreams were impossible. If I took the job, I would have to move.

A few months later, the company called and offered me the job as their first-ever remote position. All of the signs and confirmations suddenly made perfect sense—I could take the new job and stay in my current city. I knew God was calling me to make the leap of faith and take the new role. So, I did!

As I worked for the church planting company over the next year and a half, not only was I trained in how to create and run a nonprofit, but I received support in officially starting my own ministry, Embolden. I was finally able to begin building the promise I had been carrying since I was 22—rooted in my dreams where I was pregnant with a promise from God. I was finally saw more tangible fruit of promise from my 40-day fast a few years earlier.

My heart burned to see Jesus bring revival to the nations, and I wanted to lead a ministry that would help prepare God's beautiful bride from every tribe, tongue, and nation.

As I received training for my calling at my corporate job, I had a deep knowing from the Holy Spirit that I was getting prepared to launch my ministry full time. I just didn't know when the right time would come to step into this long-awaited prophetic promise.

Counting the Cost

It's easy to count the cost of taking a risk to pursue God's promises. *What could go wrong if I take a leap of faith? Will Jesus be there to catch me if things fall apart? What will I lose in pursuit of the promise?*

On the other hand, we also need to count the cost of what will happen if we *don't* move forward. The impact of your God-promise is far more reaching than you may see right now—it's about advancing God's kingdom and impacting people for his glory.

There are people you haven't met yet waiting on you to fulfill what God has created you for. If he has given you a vision to impact your family, workplace, community, city, or nation, your obedience will have a domino effect of blessing that will affect many others.

Take the wild leap of faith forward. Jesus will give you every place you set your foot.

REFLECTION

> *Now faith is the assurance of what we hope for and the certainty of what we do not see.*
> **Hebrews 11:1**

Recommended Bible Reading: Joshua 1

- What could go wrong if you pursue God's promises?
- What if you do not pursue them?
- Is God calling you to obey him this season in a way that requires bravery?

Dear Lord Jesus,

I pray for boldness and courage! Help me overcome fear with faith to conquer the territory you have for me. I pray for crystal clear confirmations that I am taking the best steps forward. I ask for you to catch me when I feel like I'm freefalling in faith. Thank you for being with me every step of the journey! Amen.

THE MIRACLE IS IN YOUR MOVEMENT

> *And as soon as the priests who carry the ark of the Lord—the Lord of all the earth—set foot in the Jordan, its waters flowing downstream will be cut off and stand up in a heap.*
> **Joshua 3:13**

One obstacle stood between God's people and their Promised Land: the Jordan River.

To cross over, God told the Israelites that the river would only part when the feet of the priests carrying the ark touched the water's edge. They needed to take a literal step of faith forward for God to open the way.

> *Now the Jordan is at flood stage all during harvest.*
> **Joshua 3:15**

Not only did they need a miracle, but they also required an *extra-strength* miracle to cross over when the waters were flooding. But if God parted the Red Sea, why couldn't he part a flooding river, too?

> *Yet as soon as the priests who carried the ark reached the Jordan and their feet touched the water's edge, the water from upstream stopped flowing.*
> **Joshua 3:15-16**

As the priests touched the waters, the river parted—just as God said. The children of Israel miraculously crossed over on dry ground. The miracle was in their movement.

Obedience, Adventure, and Faith

How often do we wait for the seemingly perfect circumstances to obey God and move forward in the things he has called us to do?

How many times have we waited for our own Jordan Rivers to part while we are still approaching from a distance?

Our God is not a boring God. He may be unconventional at times, but he is often so much more adventurous and exciting than he gets credit for. He is beckoning us to a life of faith-filled adventure.

God is not asking us to figure out exactly how he is going to perform the miracle in our lives—he's asking for our faith.

The "perfect" circumstances may never arrive—so we have to be ready and willing to move when Jesus says, "Follow me!"

He is asking us for our simple steps of obedience toward the water's edge. As we trust him and move forward, he will create a miracle in our movement, too.

PROPHETIC ENCOURAGEMENT
PIONEERS, CROSS OVER!

Pioneers, it is time to cross over into uncharted territory!

Do you feel that sense of adventure bubbling up? You can find comfort in knowing God goes before you to lead the way. Facing the roaring waters is where your faith is forged. He will release your next steps and directions to prepare you. As you move forward, the path ahead will start to clear. Like it says in Joshua 3:4, *"Then you will know which way to go, since you have never been this way before."* Remember, the miracle is in your movement. You have to get momentum going to see the miraculous moment.

We can't just be hearers of the word—we must be doers! When Jesus gives instructions about where he is taking us, we must take decisive action. It is an actionable faith that pleases God. Even if you have just a glimpse of where God is leading you, take first steps toward your promises. Don't despise the day of small beginnings. Put an end to perfectionism, procrastination, doubt, double-mindedness, and fear. Move forward, afraid, without knowing all of the details. Creating momentum will get you unstuck!

The bright future ahead of you is brimming with hope. You are called to forge a new path. Enter the Jordan and trust that God will make a way where there is no way.

As you move forward, you will find the miracle in your movement.

REFLECTION

> *But be doers of the word, and not hearers only, deceiving yourselves.*
> **James 1:22 ESV**
>
> *And without faith it is impossible to please God, because anyone who comes to him must believe that he exists and that he rewards those who earnestly seek him.*
> **Hebrews 11:6**

Recommended Bible Reading: Joshua 3

- Ask the Lord, "Are you calling me to take practical action toward my promises? If so, what are you inviting me to do?"

- Ask God, "Is there anything holding me back from taking a step toward my promises?" Pray and give anything to God that he reveals to you.

Dear Heavenly Father,

Thank you for going before me and making a way into my promised land. As I move forward, I trust you will part the way. Show me the next step, and I'll get moving in obedience! I will not delay when you call me. Help me to be strong and courageous! In Jesus' name, amen.

CROSSING MY JORDAN

> *"Now then, you and all these people, get ready to cross the Jordan River into the land I am about to give to them—to the Israelites. I will give you every place where you set your foot, as I promised Moses."*
> **Joshua 1:2-3**

"It is time to cross over!"

I was in my living room worshiping on my keyboard when I heard the phrase like a still, small thought. I was caught off guard. *What did it mean?*

I could have easily brushed off the whisper, but I knew that familiar voice. It was so familiar, so subtle that I could almost mistake it for my own thoughts at times. But I have learned to pause and listen—to discern and honor the voice of the Lord.

As I prayed into the phrase, God began to speak to me about the Israelites crossing over the Jordan River into the land of Canaan. In the same way, I felt God was now calling his people forward out of the wilderness and into their promised lands.

The very next day, my time to cross over arrived: I was unexpectedly let go from my full-time job.

After the exit interview, I cried for a few hours. And then, I felt a surprising sense of deep peace. I thought to myself, *My fear of losing my job security has kept me from doing full-time ministry! My worst fear came true— but the world didn't end! I am okay! I survived!*

There's something freeing that happens when you face your fears and make it out on the other side with Jesus. I felt empowered. Emboldened.

The loss of my job was a blessing in disguise. That day was the start of God moving me from my multi-year wilderness into my personal promised land. Looking back on that fateful February day, I'm reminded of Joshua's charge to God's people the day before they crossed the Jordan in Joshua 3:5: "Consecrate yourselves, for tomorrow the Lord will do amazing things among you."

After hearing the word of the Lord while at my keyboard, my life changed the next day. Practically overnight, years of prayers were answered. I could no longer stay in the wilderness. I had to cross over. God was calling me into full-time ministry.

I knew this prophetic promise of crossing over was not just for me. I believe it is a word for many people in this new prophetic era.

Do you hear God calling you out of the wilderness and into your promised land? Jesus will embolden us to take the land.

A Dream of Confirmation

The day I lost my job, I prayed and asked God for confirmation that going into full-time ministry was my next step. While I had already legally founded my ministry, I hadn't officially launched it. If I was going all in, my first goal would be starting an online ministry school.

When I checked my social media inbox the next morning, a friend named Cassie told me she had a dream about me that night.

"I had a dream about you that was simple and beautiful. I saw you sitting outside at a picnic table outside with strung lights above you," Cassie said. "You were near a barn, and I saw an open field before you. You were asking if the background was a good set up for the platform for the new thing you were doing, You uncertain if you were doing the right thing, and I kept telling you it was perfect for you! It was a peaceful area where you were going to start your new beginning."

Cassie's dream was an answer to my prayer. She didn't know what I had been praying about, nor did she know her dream described a coffee house I often visit to do ministry work from my laptop. I sent her a picture of the coffee house with the picnic table and strung lights, and she confirmed it was similar to the setting she saw in her dream!

In the dream, the field represented the area God was calling me to reach in ministry.. The barn represented his supernatural provision to do my calling.

The Lord was so kind to give me confirmation to encourage me to step into my prophetic promise. I decided to start pursuing my dream of full-time ministry. My feet were about to touch the water's edge of my personal Jordan.

REFLECTION

You are about to cross the Jordan to enter and take possession of the land the LORD your God is giving you.
Deuteronomy 11:31

For we are God's handiwork, created in Christ Jesus to do good works, which God prepared in advance for us to do.
Ephesians 2:10

- When have you experienced a blessing in disguise?
- What would it look like if God started fulfilling your promise tomorrow? How would you respond?
- What supernatural confirmations has Jesus encouraged you with about your promises?

Dear Lord Jesus,

Help me cross over into my promises! Thank you for your kindness in pushing me out of the nest when I need to get moving. Thank you for releasing blessings in disguise—shut and open doors of timing and opportunity—that help me to enter into my promised land. Release supernatural confirmations as I move ahead. Please order my steps directly into the prophetic promises you have for me! Amen.

KEEP THE TESTIMONY ALIVE

> *He said to the Israelites, "In the future when your descendants ask their parents, 'What do these stones mean?' tell them, 'Israel crossed the Jordan on dry ground.'*
>
> **Joshua 4:21-22**

When God performs miracles and fulfills promises in our lives, we have a responsibility to forever remember and share with others what he has done.

Upon crossing the Jordan, the Israelites took twelve memorial stones from the river to remind their children of God's faithfulness. Their stones proclaimed their miraculous testimony, "We passed over the Jordan on dry ground!"

Like the Israelites, we are called to collect our own stones of remembrance from our history with God. We can't keep a promise fulfilled to ourselves. It's a testimony for future generations that declares to them, "God is real! Jesus is faithful and true. Here's how he revealed himself to me in a personal way—and he will make himself known to you, too."

Not only that, but our witness about Jesus carries authority and creates a multiplication of fruit in the lives of others. We have experiential knowledge that God is a Waymaker and Miracle Worker. He is a Promise Maker and Promise Keeper. Sharing our testimonies prophesies to those who hear, "If God did this for me, he can do it for you too! He will reveal himself to you in a personal way."

Others will possess their own prophetic promises as they hear what God has done for us. That's why we are called to keep our testimony alive for the glory of Jesus.

One Step at a Time

At the start of my own journey to my prophetic promises, when it seemed like all of my promises were far out of reach, I had a dream about Charlie Brown and the Peanut Gallery.

I saw an invitation note card addressed to me from the Peanuts Gang. I opened it to find the cartoon characters from Charlie Brown holding up a giant sign that said, "This is never going to work!"

The dream made me worried. Did this mean the promise I had from God would never happen?

I shared the dream with a friend named Shelly, and she started laughing.

"Mariel," she said, "Don't you know what the Peanut Gallery represents? It means gossip! Have you ever heard the phrase, 'That's enough from the peanut gallery!'? God is telling you not to listen to the naysayers and those who don't believe your promises will happen! Listen to God's voice instead."

Her interpretation brought immediate relief to my heart. I began to understand that the dream message was an invitation to listen to the enemy's voice of doubt and unbelief—gossip is not from God. I didn't need to accept the invitation from the Peanut Gallery. *Return to sender.*

As I pondered her words, I heard the Lord say, "Take one step at a time, Mariel. Go to the store and buy a new journal. I want you to write down the testimonies and confirmations I will give you on the way to your promises from me. This is just the beginning."

I went to TJ Maxx and looked through the journal section, but none caught my eye. I decided to look somewhere else. Before leaving the store, I grabbed a snack and headed to check out. Standing in line, I looked over at the shelf in the checkout lane.

I couldn't believe it! Right before me, there was a spiral-bound journal with Charlie Brown's Snoopy on the cover. Printed on the front was the phrase: *ONE STEP AT A TIME!*

God confirmed his word to me. I got the journal and began to record my prophetic journey from that day onward.

Many of the testimonies in this book are the fruit of that special notebook. These pages in your hands are some of the stones marking the pathway to my prophetic promises from God.

I pray my story declares to you, "If God did this for Mariel, he will do it for me too! All of my promises are yes and amen in Jesus Christ."

REFLECTION

> *And he said to the people of Israel, "When your children ask their fathers in times to come, 'What do these stones mean?' then you shall let your children know, 'Israel passed over this Jordan on dry ground.' So that all the peoples of the earth may know that the hand of the Lord is mighty, that you may fear the Lord your God forever."*
> **Joshua 4:21-22, 24 ESV**

Recommended Bible Reading: Joshua 4

Prophetic Activation: What three testimony stones have you collected on your journey with God? Record how God has moved in your life. Write it down. Paint it as a picture. Make a collage. Get creative and commemorate the work of God in your life. Share your testimony with at least three people this week.

> *Dear Heavenly Father,*
>
> *Thank you for all of the stones of testimony you have given me! I'm so grateful for all of the ways you have led me, protected me, provided for me, and prepared me. Help me not to keep what you've done in my life to myself! Give me the boldness to share all of the miraculous testimonies you've given me so that others can know you and see what's possible with you! In Jesus' name, amen.*

TAKE THE CITY

> *The commander of the Lord's army replied, "Take off your sandals, for the place where you are standing is holy." And Joshua did so.*
> **Joshua 5:15**

When you finally cross the Jordan, you may think all of the challenges are over. The promised land should be move-in-ready ... right? On the contrary, your adventure isn't over yet. You will have to rise up to take the land.

As Joshua headed toward Jericho, the Commander of the Lord's army met him.

He was not on the enemy's side nor Joshua's side. He was there on assignment from God.

Joshua needed supernatural help to lead the nation of Israel to victory.

The enemy they faced was far too big, far too numerous.

The victory did not belong to Joshua—it belonged to God.

During this encounter, the commander of the Lord's army asked Joshua to remove his shoes.

Why did Joshua remove his shoes?

1. It represents his humility.
2. It represents his reverence for God.
3. It represents his dependence on God.
4. It represents a covenant between him and God.

As we move into our promises, we must also take our shoes off. Our promised land is holy ground. We need to acknowledge that we are in the presence of a holy God with a holy assignment. We can't take the land without his help. He will not leave us on the edge of the Jordan River. What God starts, he always finishes.

Our victory will be a sign to others that declares, "Only God could have accomplished this!"

Conquering Jericho

> *On the seventh day, they got up at daybreak and marched around the city seven times in the same manner, except that on that day they circled the city seven times.*
> **Joshua 6:15**

During his encounter with the Commander of the Lord's Armies, Joshua received specific instructions on conquering the city of Jericho.

We can often glean a prophetic message when God uses a specific number pattern in scripture.[4] This is the case in the story of the fall of Jericho where the number seven represents perfection and completion.

In Joshua chapter 6, God commands the people to march around the city led by:

- 7 priests carrying
- 7 trumpets, to march for
- 7 days, with
- 7 final marches on the 7th day

Miraculously, the walls of Jericho fell on the seventh day! God gave instructions using the number seven to orchestrate a complete and perfect victory for Joshua and the Israelites.

God's Victories

On this path to our prophetic promises, the Lord will be faithful in releasing instructions to us as we surrender to his plans.

We can sometimes struggle to discern God's voice, but I love to look at stories like Jericho and remind myself that God delights in giving *specific* instructions to his people! He will speak through signs, wonders, dreams, visions, his still small voice, and even numbers to get our attention, direct us, and make his will known to us.

While his instructions may not always make the most practical sense at first, faith begins to look logical when God starts to speak. Our acts of faith become prophetic declarations that lead to powerful breakthroughs.

Follow God's commands in obedience and watch as walls crumble that have been blocking you from conquering everything God has for you.

With Jesus on your side, anything is possible. It's time to claim your full inheritance in him.

REFLECTION

> *By faith the walls of Jericho fell, after the army had marched around them for seven days.*
> **Hebrews 11:30**

> *When the trumpets sounded, the army shouted, and at the sound of the trumpet, when the men gave a loud shout, the wall collapsed; so everyone charged straight in, and they took the city.*
> **Joshua 6:20**

Recommended Bible Reading: Joshua 6

- Are any walls or obstacles (Jericho's) standing between you and your promised land?
- Have you ever done an act of faith to see a miracle? Ask God if there is an act of faith you can do to see your walls fall.

Dear Lord Jesus,

Help me to conquer the Jericho's in my life. I ask you to release specific instructions and strategies that give me victory over my enemies. Even when your strategy requires faith, I want to conquer the land! I want every part of the promised land you have for me. Amen.

EVERY PROMISE FULFILLED

> *Not a single one of all the good promises the LORD had given to the family of Israel was left unfulfilled; everything he had spoken came true.*
> **Joshua 21:45 NLT**

After years of wandering in the wilderness, the children of Israel finally tasted the milk and honey of the Promised Land. They got to behold the pomegranates of promise.

Each of the twelve tribes of Israel received special blessings and plots of land allotted to them. God gave every tribe a beautiful, unique inheritance with boundary lines designating what belonged to each one.

As it says in Joshua 21:44, "They had rest on every side."

Their wandering, waiting, and warring for the Promised Land was finished.

The promise was no longer a whispered rumor but a present reality.

God, our faithful Promise Keeper, fulfilled every promise to his people.

Your Promised Land

There will come a day when your eyes finally see your own promised land.

Envision what it will look like and how you will feel when you cross your Jordan River.

Place the vision before you and write down every detail.

Thank God for where he is taking you before you arrive.

Thank him for every road sign and wonder marking the way forward.

Praise him in the wilderness, delay, battlefield, and refiner's fire.

As God leads you on your faith-filled adventure, I pray that your testimony will be full of beautiful fruit of promise.

Fruit that shows the world you are a disciple of Jesus.

Fruit that demonstrates God is a Promise Keeper and Fulfiller.

Fruit that leads lost and broken people to our loving heavenly Father.

I pray you hold your own pomegranates of promise in due time.

As God fulfills one promise to you, I pray he begins to birth new dreams, visions, and plans in your heart for the future—prophetic promises that keep you seeking and finding Jesus Christ with all of your heart, mind, soul, and strength.

I pray your testimony will be, "Not one of the good promises God made to me fell to the ground. Everything he promised came to pass."

My Promised Land

> *When I called, you answered me; you greatly emboldened me.*
> **Psalm 138:3**

As I prepared to step into full-time ministry, God gave me a dream. I saw a great waterfall in the middle of the ocean—a natural wonder. People of all ages, backgrounds, and ethnicities traveled to the waterfall. They were ready for a grand adventure. They came to ride the rapids on yellow rafts in their everyday clothes.

When I woke up, the Lord spoke to me and said, "I am sending people from all over the world to you to receive ministry training and discipleship to prepare my Bride for revival."

My city in Georgia has the world's largest manufactured whitewater rafting area, located on the Chattahoochee River that flows through the town. People come from around the world to ride the waves in yellow rafts. This is what the waterfall represented in my dream.

Over the past two years since I began my online ministry programs, hundreds of people from all over the world—27 countries and 40 states—have received ministry equipping through Embolden.

While people have yet to travel physically to my city where the Chattahoochee flows, they have joined me online from around the world. I have received testimonies of students hearing God and prophesying hope for the first time, leading the lost to Jesus, receiving supernatural healings, stepping into callings, breaking free from hopelessness, and so much more. Most of all, I have been honored to hear the stories of people from all over the world getting to know Jesus more intimately as a friend and experiencing the power and presence of the Holy Spirit in their lives. God has been so faithful in beginning to fulfill this incredible prophetic promise in my life, and I give Jesus all of the glory. It's been more than I could ask or imagine, and I know there is still so much more to come.

While God has begun to fulfill my long-awaited promise of a ministry calling, I am still waiting for him to complete other prophetic promises, including his love story for me—his dream of heaven-designed marriage. That is a prophetic adventure to tell for another time, another book. I suppose sharing parts of that journey with you now is my way of practicing Isaiah 54. Like Sarah, I am celebrating in faith and making room before I see my prophetic promise come to pass. As I prophetically declared in my dream about my engagement party with the cardinal of answered prayer, I say again about my promise now: "It's already written in the book!"

I want to encourage you, if you are believing for a God-ordained marriage: this is a beautiful prophetic promise I believe the Lord is releasing over this generation. He will bring together kingdom covenants that prophetically declare that Jesus is returning as our wonderful Bridegroom for his Church, his radiant Bride. These tailor-made love stories will reflect the sacrificial, passionate love he holds for his Bride. While the enemy of our souls has raged against these special marriages from coming together, Jesus will prevail. I believe that God will also release seemingly impossible marriage restoration. Get ready, because your Bridegroom may surprise you with this promise in a way and a time you may not expect—even at the midnight hour.

Through every cardinal of answered prayer, praying prophet and pomegranate of promise, and every wilderness and waiting season, God led me on a wild adventure to my prophetic promises. The exciting truth is that even more adventures with Jesus await.

The Father's Ultimate Prophetic Promise

Our own personal promised land journeys are a part of God's larger narrative. We are all awaiting the fulfillment of the greatest prophetic promise: Jesus Christ returning for his Bride.

Although no man knows the day or the hour of his coming, the Father knows. He is looking forward to the day he finally gets to tell his Son, "It's time to go get your radiant Bride!"

No matter how dark the world gets, and the signs of the times unfold—the earthquakes, famines, and wars and rumors of wars—Jesus will fulfill his promise to us.

He came for the first time as an infant in a stable, fulfilling amazing prophecies no man could accomplish in his own power.

At the last trumpet sound, he will come again—but this time, as the Lion of the tribe of Judah.

He will claim his Bride from every nation, tribe, and tongue.

In the meantime, we are called to arise and shine for such a time as this. Let us contend for the beautiful prophetic promise written in Acts 2 for our generation:

> *"'In the last days,' God says,*
> *I will pour out my Spirit on all people.*
> *Your sons and daughters will prophesy, your young men will see visions,*
> *your old men will dream dreams.*
> *Even on my servants, both men and women,*

PROPHETIC PROMISES

*I will pour out my Spirit in those days, and they will prophesy.
I will show wonders in the heavens above and signs on the earth below,
blood and fire and billows of smoke.
The sun will be turned to darkness and the moon to blood
before the coming of the great and glorious day of the Lord.
And everyone who calls on the name of the Lord will be saved."*
Acts 2:17-21

Jesus is calling us to prepare in the waiting for the ultimate prophetic promise. He will return for a beautiful Bride made ready for the surprise day of her wedding.

Let us be found ready, watching and waiting, our lamps filled with oil to meet the Bridegroom when he comes.

Let us be found faithful.

Maranatha! Come, Lord Jesus.

REFLECTION

> *For no matter how many promises God has made, they are "Yes" in Christ. And so through him the "Amen" is spoken by us to the glory of God.*
> **2 Corinthians 1:20**
>
> *He who testifies to these things says, "Yes, I am coming soon." Amen. Come, Lord Jesus.*
> **Revelation 22:20**

- Take a moment to envision your promised land again. Dream and write down every detail you have about your promises fulfilled. Record the date and pray over it.
- Write a thank you note to Jesus for all he has already done and has yet to do. In faith, stir up a heart of expectation for the promises that await you. Put it somewhere safe so you can look back on it a year from now and see how God has answered your prayers.

> *Dear Heavenly Father,*
>
> *Thank you for fulfilling every promise in due time! I pray that you will get glory from my story and that others will be inspired to believe in you as they see my faith journey. May every promise be "Yes and amen" in Jesus Christ! Amen.*

FRUIT BEARERS

> *"You did not choose me, but I chose you and appointed you so that you might go and bear fruit—fruit that will last—and so that whatever you ask in my name the Father will give you."*
>
> **John 15:16**

Every promise fulfilled is like our own personal pomegranate—the fruit of the promised land.

We no longer have to pray for it, wait for it, and hope for it. We get to fully experience the promise of God.

The words of Jesus in John 15 describe the lasting fruit that comes from abiding in him and obeying his word. Only through remaining in him can we bear the fruit of our prophetic promises. As Jesus said in John 15:5, "I am the vine and you are the branches. The one who remains in Me, and I in him, will bear much fruit. For apart from Me you can do nothing."

Our fruit speaks: we abide in him. We follow him. We are his disciples. It shows the world that we intimately know Jesus as a friend.

> *"I no longer call you servants, because a servant does not know his master's business. Instead, I have called you friends, for everything that I learned from my Father I have made known to you."*
> **John 15:15**

Our Heavenly Father receives all of the glory from the fruit of our lives because it reveals his Son to the world. You can rest in the fact that he chose you for this incredible assignment.

As others behold our fruit, it will stir a holy hunger in them to seek Jesus wholeheartedly. He has a promised land adventure waiting for them, too. We can help to guide them on their own journey.

That's how the seeds of God's kingdom are multiplied.

That's how we continually bear lasting fruit.

That's how we can make disciples.

Our fruit of promise belongs to King Jesus, and the nations are waiting to hear about what he has done.

As Jesus said in John 15:8, "This is to my Father's glory, that you bear much fruit, showing yourselves to be my disciples."

Prophetic Pomegranates and the Church

Around Rosh Hashanah, two years after my initial pomegranate dream, I had another dream.

I saw the field at the church where my pomegranate bushes grow, and a large stone rock in the middle of it. This rock exists in the field in waking life, too. On it is engraved, "The gates of hell shall not prevail," which refers to how Jesus said to Peter in Matthew 16:18 (ESV), "On this rock I will build my church, and the gates of hell shall not prevail against it."

As I approached, I saw a large golden pomegranate sitting on the rock. Gold—the color that represents being tested and tried as true through God's refining fire.

Suddenly, I saw a sweet, gray-haired woman from the church smiling, standing beside the table. There was a sign with the price of the pomegranates and bible verses next to them. The church was selling them.

I looked behind her to find an orchard of pomegranates—many people were running to claim the fruit.

The day was ending, and the pomegranates were almost all gone.

I rushed to get some pomegranates, too.

They were huge—the size of pumpkins—and unusually shaped.

The sale was going to end soon, so I had to hurry.

I had mixed feelings in the dream. *Didn't these pomegranates belong to me? Why were others taking them so freely?!*

Meanwhile, I noticed a figure in the far distance.

It was a Man.

It was the Field Owner.

It was the Farmer of the harvest.

My Father was watching over the field. He was overseeing the harvest of my pomegranates.

I heard the Father say, "Mariel, these pomegranates of promise represent the fruit of your process and testimony. These pomegranates belong to me. I am going to bring the church into our fruitful harvest. It's time for others to claim their promises. A great harvest of prophetic promises is coming that will bring me great glory. As I release promises to my people, I am building my church—and the gates of hell will not prevail against it."

REFLECTION

> *Taste and see that the Lord is good; blessed is the one who takes refuge in him.*
> **Psalm 34:8**
>
> *Let us hold unswervingly to the hope we profess,*
> *for he who promised is faithful.*
> **Hebrews 10:23**

Recommended Bible Reading: John 15

- What does it mean to you that you are a friend of God?
- Who can you share your fruit with as a testimony when your prophetic promise is fulfilled (Your family, your field, etc.)?

Dear Heavenly Father,

Make me fruitful, Lord. I want to bear the fruit of being a disciple of Jesus. I want my life to display the fruit of answered prayer. Come and tend to me as my Good Gardener. Have your way in my life. Prune me, refine me, and make me ready for the harvest you have prepared for me. Let me sow seeds of promise for others to reap a harvest, too! I pray that all of my fruit will bring you great glory. In Jesus' name, amen.

OUR TRUE TREASURE

> *"The kingdom of heaven is like treasure hidden in a field.*
> *When a man found it, he hid it again, and then in his joy went and sold all he*
> *had and bought that field."*
> **Matthew 13:44**

At the start of this adventure, we may begin by seeking a prophetic promise from God.

However, the more we seek God's promise and plan, the more we find the True Treasure hidden in the field.

Every sign, wonder, and miracle is meant to lead us directly to the greatest desire we can ever fathom. Through it all, Jesus Christ becomes the ultimate prize of our hearts. He takes his rightful first place in our lives.

We discover he was constantly wooing and pursuing us in the wilderness of wonders. He was drawing us near with the tender whisper of his voice.

We find him as the fourth man in the fire, the One helping us persevere through the tests and trials of our journey.

Every promise fulfilled becomes secondary to encountering the kindness of our Hero, our Bridegroom, our King.

As we experience Jesus through every high and low, we are met by his constant faithfulness.

We experience his compassion in our moments of disappointment.

We find his gentleness in our moments of heartache and longing.

He is the one holding the pomegranate, the prophetic promise.

As we reach out our hand to take what he freely gives, we just have to look up.

There he is, with eyes of blazing fire.

He is passionate about you.

He will go to the ends of the earth for you.

He thought you were to die for.

The signs and wonders become treasures on a map that lead you to him on the way to your prophetic promises. And yes—he still has those fulfilled promises for you. It will be exceedingly and abundantly beyond your wildest imagination.

Yet, the end goal is no longer merely possessing the prophetic promise.

Our prize is finding Jesus Christ—our Ultimate Treasure.

At the end of it all, when we finally see him face to face, we get to offer the fruit of promise back to him. Like the elders casting their crowns before the throne, we get to cast our crowned pomegranates at the feet of our beautiful Bridegroom Jesus. He is worthy of all of the glory.

> *They cast their crowns before the throne, saying, "Worthy are you, our Lord and God, to receive glory and honor and power, for you created all things, and by your will they existed and were created."*
> **Revelation 4:10-11 ESV**

Remember: Jesus is not only your Promise Maker—he is your Promise Fulfiller.

He knows you intimately.

He loves you infinitely.

He is your Exceedingly Great Reward.

REFLECTION

After this, the word of the LORD came to Abram in a vision: "Do not be afraid, Abram. I am your shield, your very great reward."
Genesis 15:1

One thing I ask from the Lord, this only do I seek: that I may dwell in the house of the Lord all the days of my life, to gaze on the beauty of the Lord and to seek him in his temple.
Psalm 27:4

- Write a list of ways you have encountered Jesus on your adventure to your prophetic promises.
- What have you learned about God from your journey? What have you learned about yourself?
- What truths do you want to engrave on your heart from this adventure?

Dear Lord Jesus,

Thank you for being the Ultimate Treasure on the adventure to my prophetic promises. Help me find you in the major milestones and small details in my life. I pray for an even deeper, intimate relationship with you! I want to seek you first and know you more and more. I claim the promise that as I seek you with my whole heart, I will find you. Amen.

AFTERWARD
THE FINAL SIGN OF THE CARDINAL

> *Call to me and I will answer you and tell you
> great and unsearchable things you do not know.*
> **Jeremiah 33:3**

As I finished this book, I prayed and asked God to confirm any writing I should add, remove, or keep in its message.

The night I completed my final edits, I was taking a walk with my roommate, Katherine, when we noticed a commotion in the neighbor's yard. I looked and saw a small baby bird fighting for its life as it fended off a cat. My instincts kicked in, and I ran to protect the little bird. It was wounded beneath its wings.

I ushered the injured baby bird into a small cardboard box while our neighbor took the cat. We searched for a nest, but couldn't find one nearby. I decided to take the bird back to our porch to keep it safe, praying it would live through the night.

The next morning, I awoke to a wonderful surprise.

Katherine said, "Mariel, you won't believe this, but the baby bird you rescued was a cardinal. What's more is its mother and father found it, and the mom has been feeding the bird beak to beak this morning!"

I looked out the window to see a brown female cardinal flying around our porch, with a bright red male cardinal watching from the nearby tree. I could see the baby bird still in the cardboard box, happy and fully alive. To me, it was a miracle.

After a little while, I checked the box again, and the baby bird had found the strength to spread its wings and fly away.

I was amazed—I knew it was a sign from God. It was the final message to include in this book.

The cardinal is the sign of answered prayer.

As we call to God, he will answer us. He is watching over his word to perform it. He has a plan to bring the answers to our prayers. He has a plan to fulfill his promises.

If Jesus takes care of the birds, how much more does he take care of us? Though our cardinals, our answered prayers, may be battered and bruised from the battle of faith, they are still alive and well. Though the promises of God have gone through the refiner's fire, they will come forth as gold.

The cardinal also represents the revival of promises and dreams from God that have died and are coming back to life. The cardinals,

AFTERWARD

the prodigals and Jonah's, are coming home. The lost are being found. Your prophetic promise will experience the resurrection power of Jesus Christ.

Let this be a prophetic sign to you—the cardinals are coming.

Keep praying and prophesying your promises.

Your answered prayers are on the way—they are already taking flight.

> *The LORD said to me, "You have seen correctly,*
> *for I am watching to see that my word is fulfilled."*
> **Jeremiah 1:12**

A PRAYER OF SURRENDER

Dear Heavenly Father,

I want to surrender my whole life to you, Lord. I acknowledge you in all my ways and lay down my own understanding. I invite you to direct all of my paths (Proverbs 3:5-6). I don't want to go my own way, Jesus. I want to lose my life so I can find true life in you. I want to possess every beautiful promise written in your will for me.

I pray that you shut the wrong doors in my life and open the right ones you have for me. Prepare me for the wonderful blessings you want to give me. Make my life a living, burning sacrifice that delights in doing your will. Do whatever it takes, God. I give you permission to be the Good Gardener in my life who prunes me to help me grow and become fruitful for your kingdom (John 15). Help me to obey all of your words.

Please take my life and use it for your glory. Write me a beautiful story that only the Good Author and Finisher can dream up. Thank you for taking every difficulty and using it all for my good and to accomplish your purposes in and through my life. Thank you that your precious blood covers all of the pain of my past. It is finished.

Lord, I ask that you give me a heart that burns for you. Set me ablaze with your love so I can't help but overflow with love for others and show the world who you are through my life. I hold nothing back from you, God. Be Lord over every area of my life. Here I am. Send me! (Isaiah 6:8)

In the mighty name of Jesus, I pray, amen.

ACKNOWLEDGEMENTS

First, I would like to thank my sweet angel mother, Suzanne. When I was little, I remember following you around our house from room to room as you opened every blind every morning, letting the light in. Mom, you always let the light in. You are always there to speak hope, wisdom, and faith to your daughters. You are the definition of strength to me in so many ways. Thank you for all your love and sacrifice as a single mom raising two young girls. It's because of you that I have any wisdom to share with the world. You are the reason I have a faith built on the Rock. You have been there in every season, and I am grateful to have a mom like you. Love you mom!

Thank you to my faithful friend and intercessor, Katherine Server. Thank you for being there to pray with me and encourage me, especially in delivering this book. Many of these "word treasure" wonders and adventures were experienced with you right there to witness the work of Jesus in my life. You are truly an Elizabeth to my Mary. I am grateful for you!

I also want to thank my sister, Suzanna, and my family for all of their support. To my friends in the Columbus community and FCC family, I am so grateful for you.

Thank you to my prophetic school students and mentorship mentees for pursuing Jesus wholeheartedly with me.

Thank you to every person who has supported and prayed for the ministry—to see the Gospel of Jesus Christ go forth and the word of the Lord "run swiftly and be glorified."

Lastly, I would like to thank Jesus, my faithful Bridegroom. I don't have words to fully express, Lord, what you have meant to me. You are worthy of all my costly perfume being poured out. Thank you for giving me so much precious oil on my journey with you so I can continue to have more to pour out at your feet. Let the fragrance of the Rose of Sharon fill the room. You're my everything.

Where You go, I will go.

Where You stay, I will stay.

I love you, King Jesus.

NOTES

The Power of a Prophetic Promise

1. "Greek Lexicon entry for G1097 - ginosko." *Strong's Concordance*. *Blue Letter Bible*. Accessed March 20, 2024.
2. Guzik, David. "Study Guide for John 10." *Blue Letter Bible*. Accessed May 7, 2024. https://www.blueletterbible.org/comm/guzik_david/study-guide/john/john-10.cfm.
3. See 1 John 3:19-24.
4. See 1 Kings 19:11-13
5. Vilhauer, Jennice Ph.D. "How Your Thinking Creates Your Reality." *Psychology Today*, September 28, 2020. Accessed April 18, 2024. https://www.psychologytoday.com/us/blog/living-forward/202009/how-your-thinking-creates-your-reality.
6. Ref. 1 Corinthians 14:1-3.
7. "Greek Lexicon entry for prophéteuó (prof-ate-yoo'-o)." *Strong's Concordance*. *Blue Letter Bible*. Accessed March 20, 2024.
8. Vallotton, Kris. "The Goal of the Gift of Prophecy." *Kris Vallotton Ministries*, accessed April 18, 2024. https://www.krisvallotton.com/the-goal-of-the-gift-of-prophecy.

Our Promise Maker

1. Buehler, Dr. Juergen. "The Tower of the Flock." *International Christian Embassy of Jerusalem*. Accessed April 12, 2024. https://www.icej.org/blog/the-tower-of-the-flock/

Wilderness Wonders

1. "Hebrew Lexicon entry for H4057 - מִדְבָּר (midbar)." *Strong's Concordance. Blue Letter Bible.* Accessed May 12, 2024.
2. "Hebrew Lexicon entry for H226 - תוא (owth)." *Strong's Concordance. Blue Letter Bible.* Accessed April 12, 2024.
3. "Hebrew Lexicon entry for H6382 - אֶלֶף (pele)." *Strong's Concordance. Blue Letter Bible.* Accessed April 12, 2024.
4. "Hebrew Lexicon entry for H4478 - מָן (manna)." *Strong's Concordance. Blue Letter Bible.* Accessed March 20, 2024.
5. "Mantis." *Etymology Online.* Accessed March 20, 2024. https://www.etymonline.com/word/mantis.
6. Brewer, Troy. *Numbers That Preach: Understanding God's Mathematical Lingo.* Aventine Press, 2007.
7. "Confirm." *Merriam-Webster Dictionary,* accessed April 30, 2024, https://www.merriam-webster.com/dictionary/confirm.
8. "Hebrew Lexicon entry for H3290 - בקעי (Jacob)." *Strong's Concordance. Blue Letter Bible.* Accessed April 14, 2024.

Just in Time

1. "Hebrew Lexicon entry for H3485 - רככשי (Yissaskar)." *Strong's Concordance. Blue Letter Bible.* Accessed March 20, 2024.
2. "Ancient Jewish Wedding Customs and Yeshua's Second Coming," *Bibles for Israel,* accessed April 29, 2024, https://free.messianicbible.com/feature/ancient-jewish-wedding-customs-and-yeshuas-second-coming/.
3. Robert R. Cargill, PhD., "Meaning, origin and history of the name Esther," *Behind the Name,* accessed April 11, 2024, https://www.behindthename.com/name/esther.

Stay the Course

1. "Counterfeit." *Merriam-Webster Dictionary.* Accessed April 12, 2024. https://www.merriam-webster.com/dictionary/counterfeit.
2. "Greek Lexicon entry for G1253 - diakrisis." *Strong's Concordance. Blue Letter Bible.* Accessed April 12, 2024.
3. "Hebrew Lexicon entry for H8050 - לאומש (Samuel)." Strong's Concordance. Blue Letter Bible. Accessed March 20, 2024.
4. "Hebrew Lexicon entry for H7136 - הָרָק (qarah)." Strong's Concordance. Blue Letter Bible. Accessed March 20, 2024.

NOTES

Gold Refined by Fire

1. "Hebrew Lexicon entry for H2472 - לְאָרְשִׁי (Israel)." *Strong's Concordance. Blue Letter Bible.* Accessed April 14, 2024.
2. "Hebrew Lexicon entry for H6293 - פָגַע (paga)." Strong's Concordance. Blue Letter Bible. Accessed April 26, 2024.
3. Harper, Douglas. "Cardinal (n.)." *Online Etymology Dictionary*, 2022. https://www.etymonline.com/word/cardinal.
4. "Greek Lexicon entry for G2573 - kalos." *Strong's Concordance. Blue Letter Bible.* Accessed March 20, 2024.

Enter the Promised Land

1. "Hebrew Lexicon entry for H7416 - וֹמֵּר (rimmon)." *Strong's Concordance. Blue Letter Bible.* Accessed April 15, 2024.
2. Sobel, Jason. *Aligning with God's Appointed Times.* Rjs Publishing, 2020.
3. "Bursting with Fruitfulness." *One for Israel.* Accessed April 15, 2024. https://www.oneforisrael.org/bible-based-teaching-from-israel/bursting-with-fruitfulness/.
4. Brewer, Troy. *Numbers That Preach: Understanding God's Mathematical Lingo.* Aventine Press, 2007.

ABOUT THE AUTHOR

Mariel Villarreal

Mariel is a writer, speaker, and prophetic voice. In July 2021, she founded The Embolden Company, a ministry dedicated to bringing revival to the nations. Through Embolden, she holds online prophetic schools, mentorships, retreats, and conferences for people all over the world to hear God with confidence for their lives and the world around them.
She is from Columbus, Georgia, and she is the proud dog mom of a mini cockapoo, Sebastian.

WWW.MARIELVILLARREAL.COM

FOLLOW MARIEL

Instagram: @Mariel_Villarreal_

Tiktok: @Mariel.Villarreal

Facebook: @theemboldencompany

Youtube: Youtube.com/marielspeaks

Website: www.MarielVillarreal.com

DO YOU HAVE A TESTIMONY?

We'd love to hear how this book impacted you. Scan to share your story, sign up for my newsletter, and learn more about Embolden Co.!

Made in the USA
Monee, IL
12 August 2024